FLOATING WEST

FLOATING WEST

The Erie and Other American Canals

RUSSELL BOURNE

W · W · NORTON & COMPANY

NEW YORK · LONDON

Library of Congress Cataloging in Publication Data

Bourne, Russell.
        Floating America west: the Erie and other American canals / by
Russell Bourne.
                p.   cm.
        Includes bibliographical references.
                1. Canals—United States—History.   I. Title.
        HE395.A3B68   1992
        386'.4'0973—dc20   91-30065

ISBN 0–393–03044–X

W. W. Norton & Company, Inc., 500 Fifth Avenue, New York, N.Y. 10110
W. W. Norton & Company Ltd., 10 Coptic Street, London WC1A 1PU

1 2 3 4 5 6 7 8 9 0

To Mother

S. R. B.

CONTENTS

Illustrations follow pages 72 and 136

INTRODUCTION

WALTER EDMONDS, author of *Rome Haul* and laureate of New York's Mohawk Valley, wrote that one Irish immigrant ditchdigger asked another: "What do they want this canal for, anyway?" In another place in the same book, a character named O'Mory remarks to his comrades: "Ye've built the thing. It's whome to ye." And that remark almost answers the first question, for New York's Erie Canal was supposed to create a new, desirable homeland for all sorts and conditions of people. It was also to unite a nation—to take the people to the glories of the West. Both of those historic objectives (and many more) were accomplished by the 1825 completion of the "Great Western," as contemporaries liked to call the canal. But far more attention has been paid to the second accomplishment than to the first.

As well as examining the technology of the canal and its predecessors, this book therefore pays special attention to the opening up of that new homeland—from long before the American Revolution to today, when the Erie and other once-vital American canals are serving as prime recreation areas. The book celebrates many heroes (led by De Witt Clinton, "Magnus Apollo") and discovers a number of villains (led by Martin Van Buren, "Red Fox of Kinderhook") along the way. It marks many special events, such as the completion exactly two hundred years ago (1791) of the first successful locks at Little Falls, which anticipated the locks of the Erie (and whose successors are still visible today). It introduces the engineers and balladeers, the barge captains and lock tenders who helped make up the cast of characters along the Erie Canal and other canals that developed in the wake of the Erie. It raises a question—how did these transported Americans like their new home and modernized society, their "West," once the canals had led them there? That is, were they then better able to pursue happiness?

The answer is fascinatingly mixed. The riches that flowed as a result of this new, water-powered economy were vast, the political effects revolutionary. In the words of Samuel Eliot Morison, "The Erie Canal, completed [in 1825], made New York the Empire State," changing it from a wilderness to the nation's mightiest state. And yet the impact of that political and economic advance on the lower classes was by no means totally beneficial. As perceived by James Truslow Adams, "The new transportation facilities . . . rapidly transformed the position and character of labor." The American farmhand gained much but lost self-reliance when he took employment at a mill powered by the new waterway. He—and all Americans along with him—became part of the industrialized, corporate system that would, among other things, lose a balanced relationship with nature and win the Civil War for the North.

Because of the lead role played by the Erie Canal in America's waterborne entrance to the Age of Progress, the three central chapters of the book are devoted to that canal's history, construction, and social consequences. The first chapter positions this drama in the total story of post-Revolutionary American development; the fifth looks at the proliferation of other canals and describes the use of canals for recreational purposes today.

Drivers along the New York State Thruway occasionally glimpse some of the old Erie's out-of-time ruins, not quite carcasses of dinosaurs but fossils similarly removed from us by incomprehensible eons. These eroding canal ruins—beautifully built aqueducts, arches, locks—seem to be disappearing gently into the land, making no claim to relevance or historical importance. Yet the thruway itself is figuratively built upon those ruins; it would not be there without those antecedents. For canals were the grandfathers of all long-distance transportation systems on this continent. A trucker roaring down the thruway lets loose a blast on his air horn and quite appropriately gives a comradely wave to the young couple boating up the New York State Barge Canal, which now runs where once the Erie ran.

Although this book is not structured as a guide—I hope that it will help travelers by both land and water to appreciate more fully the mystical, genius-filled land through which they move. And for the very fact that they are moving at all, credit should be given to the Erie, which showed the way to our mobile society. Walter Edmonds called it "the unpent joy of moving."

Russell Bourne, *Litchfield, Connecticut*

FLOATING WEST

Chapter One

THE DREAM OF WATERWAYS WEST

NARROW ENOUGH to be crossed by a felled tree, American canals of the last century still slip quietly through the land in easy conspiracy with the contours. Increasing thousands of Americans discover in these old canals recreational opportunities and chances to wonder about construction techniques and people of not long ago—the evolution of our technological society. Did canals have anything to do with the way we turned and grew as people, and is that why we find these sinuous paths across the land so hauntingly familiar?

Yes, they are built into our memories in the forms of myths, songs of heroes: George Washington, De Witt Clinton; *Drums Along the Mohawk* and "Low Bridge, Everybody Down." So when one or another of these abandoned canals is rewatered and comes to life again, we feel a special joy, a reclamation of the body as well as the spirit. To float along the greatest of these canals, the Erie (now called the New York State Barge Canal), is to find hamlets and animals that we suspected all along were ours but had been lost.

George Washington called canals "fundamental to nationhood." Without such waterways, the young republic would not advance to its full potential—or even continue to exist as an integrated political unit.

13

The strategical issue was, which part of North America would control the other parts? That is, since most of the continent remained in the hands of the English and the French and the Spanish, did that mean that the newly liberated, English-speaking East Coast of the allegedly United States would always be in the shadow of the European west and north and south? Not if adequate transportation systems could be devised and routes to the Ohio Valley successfully claimed by a more rapidly expanding nation.

One of the general's first undertakings after his triumphant return from the American Revolution to Mount Vernon on Christmas Eve in 1783 was to journey west to visit his lands along (West) Virginia's Kanawha River. This mountain-cleaving torrent, leading to the Ohio River, seemed an obvious route for those who would develop westward transportation systems. Its headwaters were but 35 miles from those of the James River, which flowed directly to the Atlantic. Surely a canal link could be effected here.

In this era before the purchase of the Louisiana territories, what pressed particularly on the mind of our leading citizen-soldier was the fate of the Ohio-Michigan region. "The Western States hang upon a pivot," Washington wrote; "the touch of a feather will turn them either way." He would do what he could to see to it that the potentially magnificent harvest from this new region be shipped not down the Ohio and Mississippi to New Orleans for the benefit of the foreign merchants there but to such established East Coast cities as Richmond and Georgetown.

When Washington's projected trip to the Kanawha had to be postponed because of Indian unrest, he turned his thoughts to the Potomac as another possible way to reach and claim the Ohio. Determined to refamiliarize himself with this route, which he had first explored (to his peril) during the French and Indian Wars, he headed west to the headquarters of the river. Then he continued over the Alleghenies and down the Monongahela to the frontier settlement of Pittsburgh. From there he went on by boat down the Ohio and finished the 650-mile expedition by traveling up the Kanawha, crossing the mountains to his home valley near White Sulphur Springs.

On the basis of this tour, Washington concluded that the Potomac was, after all, the best route for the canal that would bind the continental country together. In 1785 he accepted the post of president of the "Patowmack Company" (which had been established before the Revolution) and declined the invitation to be president of the James River Company. But in these considerations, the visionary "Father of Our Country" overlooked a number of factors. America then lacked all three ingredients necessary for successful canal-building: adequate capital, technical skill (we had neither engineers nor geologists), and a work force or technology able to carry out the work. Furthermore, Washington misunderstood how to go about canal-building; he put his trust, unwisely, in improved riverways.

Yet fundamentally, he was correct. It was canals, however built, that would first bind the nation together and enable us to advance from a delimited, undeveloped country to one of the reckonable world powers of the industrial revolution. More than that, when the great canal systems of Maryland, Pennsylvania, and New York finally succeeded in effecting the link to the interior territories of the nation, another kind of revolution, a social revolution, came about. Tragically, this social revolution was not won without cost (if one ever is), nor did everyone benefit—as narrated, region by region, in the following chapters. Nonetheless, historian James McGregor Burns states without qualification that the New Yorkers of 1817–25 who completed the exemplary Erie Canal altered "the whole pattern of economic and social development" in the United States.

It was indeed the canals that shaped us, by linking us economically and empowering us politically; by giving us new heroes, new victims, new songs of work and diversion. Although it's dangerous to edge into psychohistory, Dr. Carl Jung did write of a "transcendent function," a symbolic realization in the human mind that reflects a physical form. The realization of the form enables an individual to unite his conscious with his unconscious and to fulfill his individual destiny. So it happened here: the transcendent function of the canal, the transcendent event of the uniting of our inland seas with our ocean ports, was powerful enough to inspire a generation of realized Americans, whose inspired works can be seen in architecture, religion, engineering, politics, painting; suddenly an advanced civilization appeared in the wilds of North America.

The slender, mostly unwatered remains of historic canals bely their own importance when one discovers them here or there upon the land. But this book seeks to reclaim that grandeur—to demonstrate that canals were the root and the stem of the national emergence that occurred between 1820 and 1850.

The True Power of Canals

George Washington and his Patowmack Company cannot be accused of having failed to accomplish their westward objectives for want of effort. A former military surveyor and engineer, Washington read all the technical papers he could find or order at home or abroad on the subject of old and new canals. These were, after all, the transportation systems that were carrying Great Britain to enviable heights of power as leader of the industrial revolution at the end of the eighteenth century. Washington commanded to his side anyone who, returned from Europe, might shed light on the most advanced means of construction.

Meanwhile, work on the Patowmack Canal went forward. For seven exhausting years, black slaves and white laborers (called "navvies" in England, for navigation workers) constructed a series of five locks, blasted out of the rocks at Great Falls. They also built a canal ¾ mile long around Little Falls. These improvements allowed the riverboats of the day, either poled or sail-powered, to make successful passages far upriver—if the Potomac did not happen to be suffering from one of its frequent floods or from winter ice. Yet when the Patowmack Company's projects were completed in 1802, three years after President Washington's death, even their staunchest supporters had to admit that the big step toward the West had not been taken. The mountain fastness remained firm; the great Virginian's dream of surmounting the Alleghenies was clearly beyond American capabilities in the eighteenth century.

Yet Washington never stopped hoping that somehow the means of fulfilling the dream could be found; his passionate belief in the feasibility of waterways west might even be called an obsession. When James Madison visited Mount Vernon after the President's retirement, he found the nation's hero still totally absorbed in the cause of canals. Madison wrote to Thomas Jefferson that the "earnestness" with which Washington continued to support the blasting of navigable channels and the building of locks and canals was so intense as "hardly to be described."

Transportation modes alternative to canals were, it must be pointed out, not particularly attractive at that time. Although turnpikes and "post roads" could be found in populated sections of the young republic, these were nothing more than deeply rutted dirt roads, impossible to use in the mud seasons, impractical to build across rugged distances, and expensive for freight carriers because of teamsters' costs. Macadamized roads—the 1815 invention of Scotland's John McAdam by which small stones are compacted together upon a solid stone base to provide an all-weather surface—would not come to the United States until another generation had passed. And although wooden and iron-topped rails existed (mostly for industry) in various locations, with carts towed along them by horse, railroads for heavy freight would not become feasible here until the late 1820s.

But the President's commitment to the cause of canals was not simply a matter of there being nothing better. He shared with the inventive Robert Fulton and other creative minds of the day the conviction that canals possessed an almost magical power to irrigate and inspire the land. Fulton's treatise on the subject had been sent to the President shortly before his retirement, in 1796. The stated purpose of the treatise was to "Exhibit the Certain Mode of Giving Agriculture to every Area of the emmense [sic] Continent of America, By means of A Creative System of Canals." Fulton predicted that America's much-needed canals would one day "pass through every vale, wind round each hill, and bind the whole country together in the bonds of social intercourse." And he spoke with authority, for he had been to England and seen the future happening.

Young Fulton had, in fact, been sent to England in order to study art, bearing letters of introduction to the proper galleries and personages from Benjamin Franklin, among others. Arrived in London in 1790, he gained some recognition for his painting but even more fortunately won an introduction to Francis Egerton, the 2nd Duke of Bridgewater. This venturesome nobleman, born in 1736, had grasped that there was but one way to reduce the sizable costs of moving coal from his pits at Worsley to the new industrial city of Manchester: by canal. And he had had the courage to risk his entire fortune on that concept; his gamble gained him leadership of England's industrial age.

Fascinated by the duke and his canals, Robert Fulton abandoned art to journey for eighteen months among the constructions of Egerton and

17

his engineers. On the strength of his researches, Fulton could quip know-
ingly that the Duke of Bridgewater's perception of the importance of
canals had brought him "immortality and $130,000 a year."

Nor was Fulton the only American to be impressed by the duke and
his economic advances. Surveyors sent by the New York State canal commissioners in 1817 came with notebooks to marvel at the "Wonder of the
Age," the Bingley five-rise locks designed by Egerton's engineer, James
Brindley. But of the canals built during this period, the one with the
greatest influence on the Erie was the 93-mile, seventy-four-lock Trent
and Mersey, completed in 1766. This one seemed nearly continental,
encouraging canal planners to dream on.

Fulton also realized during his longish stay among the booming, not
always pleasant realities of England's industrialized cities that there were
human and political consequences of this canal-induced prosperity. He
wrote that he was focusing on "canal navigation *as connected with political
economy.*" While Washington was primarily interested in the commercial
and nation-building potentialities of canals (as well as in their technologies), Fulton considered the ways in which canals stimulated the citizens—the ways in which new groups were given wealth and power while
other groups lost wealth and power even amid the general prosperity.

In Fulton's treatise, however, he gave little thought to the possible
negative effects of the new industrialization. Instead he devoted much
space to the justification of canals as facilitators, as history-proved means
of exploiting a nation's own interior strengths. He wrote that

it is worthy of observation that in these countries where canals were most in use
[he was describing Egypt, China, and India], they never encouraged foreign
commerce, but seem to have arrived at their great opulence by a home trade,
circulated through their extensive and numerous navigations.

Although Robert Fulton later won wealth and reputation as the creative force behind America's first commercially successful steam vessel, he
remained committed to canals as the way to crack open the way West—
and perhaps to induce a new kind of "opulent," self-sufficient civilization.
Shortly before his untimely death in 1815, Fulton wrote to the governor
of New York, putting his substantial weight behind the proposal for a
canal to connect the Great Lakes with the Hudson at Albany. His support
helped bring the Erie Canal into being.

A Matter of Hydraulics

Another visionary American who responded to Washington's call to help overcome the problems of building canals here and now was a single-minded "Yankee-Yorker" named Elkanah Watson. In 1785, at the very time when the president of the Patowmack Company was contemplating with discouragement his primitive, rock-carved locks around the river's falls, Watson came to visit him, bearing tales of discoveries among the sophisticated canals of France and Holland. Perhaps there would be some hydraulic concepts here that might be helpful for the nation-binding venture.

Elkanah Watson had begun life under rather humble circumstances, an indentured servant in the home of the wealthy Moses Brown family of Providence. But because of his excellent memory and apparent trustworthiness, he soon gained employment as a courier among the leadership of the American Revolution. Sent back and forth between the capital in Philadelphia and Ambassador Benjamin Franklin's residence in Paris, he first admired then became a student of the well-executed canals he saw in his journeys. Initially he was "fascinated by the Dutch canal system," its engineering and its efficiency; then, in France, both he and Franklin marveled at the magnificence and capacity of the famous Canal du Midi. Today this extraordinary canal, built under Louis XIV, still carries ship traffic across the midsection of France (hence its name), from the Atlantic to the Mediterranean. It is further described below.

The difference between the various European systems merits explanation—an explanation which Watson may have presumed to deliver to the President. The Dutch systems consisted of what are generally called "lateral canals," that is, canals that connect two bodies of water within the same drainage basin. Between the connected bodies, the current quite naturally flows from the higher to the lower, providing water deep enough for the passage of canal boats. That's by contrast with "summit-level" canals, which, like the Canal du Midi, must pass over a watershed between drainage basins—giving hydraulic engineers the problem of how to get water to that high point. The solution, of course, is to bring water in from some even higher point, via a channel that might have to span a considerable distance.

Most often, lateral canals are found in low-lying areas such as the coastal sands of the Netherlands and China or the delta site of Babylon or the deserts of Egypt. Of these early lateral canals, those of China may have been the most remarkable, running at their fullest development 1,115 miles from Hanchow to Peking. When Marco Polo reported this engineering wonder to the thirteenth-century Venetian court, he evidently comprehended both the canals' economic benefits and their strategic and political consequences. Not only could vast quantities of corn and rice be shipped with ease from one part of the khan's empire to another as the market dictated, but also the khan could effectively assert his authority throughout the interior by routing warships up or down the canals. As reported by Marco, the ruler had had the canals dug so that the imperial vessels could "pass from one river to the other . . . without making any part of the voyage by sea."

The narrative of Marco's travels was the best-read secular book of Europe's Middle Ages; it may well have fueled the imaginings of the princes of northern Italy. For soon these would-be kings were commanding their engineers to build aqueducts, locks, and impoundments for canals in furtherance of their military objectives. Although the classical Romans had had some successes with canals (and some failures, too—Nero had flunked his attempt to build a canal from Rome to Naples), this sudden mania for canals during the early Renaissance was unparalleled in all Italian history.

The brains behind this effort belonged chiefly to two engineers, Bertola da Novato and Leonardo da Vinci. Under the command of their patron, the Duke of Milan, da Novato constructed the summit-level Bereguardo Canal (1485), which had to climb 80 feet from valley to ridgetop. It was the first Italian canal to overcome a significant gradient. Leonardo, for his part, is generally credited with the design of the Bereguardo's key feature, its eighteen locks.

As Elkanah Watson and George Washington continued to discuss the great engineering feats seen or heard of in Europe, Watson undoubtedly gave a detailed description of Leonardo's locks. For they were as beautiful as inspired engineering can be, double-gated and mitered: the two gates of the lock came together to form a V, pointing upstream; as the pressure of the water pushed against that V, the mitered gates simply pressed more firmly against each other, preventing any water from coming into the chamber behind.

In the design of a typical lock, one of these sets of double gates would be positioned at the downstream end and another at the upstream end of the chamber, both with their points aimed upstream. A downstream-bound boat would enter the lock through the upper gate, with the water in the chamber at the same level as the upper river. Then, when the first gate had been closed behind it, the boat would be lowered down by letting water out of the chamber through valves at the base of the lower gate. Finally, when the water level had been brought down to that of the lower river the gates could be opened and the boat allowed to pass out. For a boat headed upstream, the process would be repeated in reverse.

Leonardo's locks stood in radical contrast to the medieval locks of Holland and the Low Countries. There the gates consisted of huge plank constructions that rose or fell dangerusly in gigantic guillotine-like frames. In England, the early builders of river improvements had contented them-selves with "flash locks"—a gate in a dam that could be opened by lower-ing or turning a "paddle." (Curiously, this simple system resembled the far more sophisticated "bear-trap" locks invented for Pennsylvania's Le-high Canal in the 1830s; see Chapter 5). But when the pound lock with mitered gate was introduced to England in the seventeenth century, that nation accepted it as a tremendous advance; now England was empow-ered to take the lead into the new age of canal-based industry.

It was in seventeenth-century France, however, that Leonardo's revo-lutionary locks made their greatest immediate impact.

The Magnificent Canal du Midi

The scene of the first French canal triumph had been upon the divide separating the watershed of the Seine River from that of the Loire River. In 1642, French engineers were able to sling the Canal de Briare across this ridge, utilizing some forty-one of Leonardo's double-gated mitered locks. The canal was large-scaled, capacious enough to allow not only barges but also ships to pass from one of these major rivers to the other, a passage of 34 miles. This premier summit-level canal worked effectively and throughout most of the year, both because it received adequate water from a higher source and because flood danger was banished by its run-ning not in a riverway but in its own channel.

Yet it was not the Canal de Briare but the subsequent masterpiece, the

Canal du Midi (1666–81), that captured the attentions of Elkanah Watson, Benjamin Franklin, Thomas Jefferson, and a host of other Americans who came to find a continental model for the accomplishment of their westward dreams. When Watson examined the canal near the end of the American Revolution, he could not but be struck by the fact that it had been a monarch—Louis XIV—who has had the might to turn this grand-scaled vision into a reality. The vision of constructing an artificial channel through the midsection of France, in between the Pyrenees to the south and the Massif Central to the north, had originally been glimpsed by a country gentleman named Pierre Paul Riquet. He ultimately persuaded Louis's brilliant finance minister, Jean Baptiste Colbert, that the idea of helping ships sail overland from the Atlantic to the Mediterranean was practicable and deserved funding.

Riquet's interests in the project were not only (as he professed) to aid the king in bringing the country together but also to benefit his own native region, Languedoc, through which the canal would pass. For centuries this wild southern region had been known for its otherness, its antipathies to both church and crown. Its very name differentiated it from the more populous north. *Langue d'Oc,* the original spelling, means "language of Oc," *oc* being a regional word for "yes." The northern part of the kingdom, by contrast, spoke the *Langue d'Ouil*—*ouil* being the way *oui* was then spelled. Was this benighted region the proper recipient of royal largess?

In Languedoc, brigands roamed the countryside. Protestants, whose religion would soon be banned by Louis's revocation of the Edict of Nantes (1685), found hideaways in these hidden valleys. Perhaps the king and Colbert had thought that a way to subdue the rebellious region was to upgrade it by means of Riquet's ambitous project. The improved transportation system would so improve agriculture and increase industry (if you listened to Riquet) that all would prosper. And perhaps Riquet, if controlled by incentives and specifications, could actually get the work done on time and see that contractors adhered to engineering standards set by the crown, Colbert may have thought. As for Riquet's incentive: in addition to the usual number of titles and honors, he would receive in perpetuity a percentage of assessments on the salt transported on the canal. That should satisfy him.

It did indeed—Riquet's heirs eventually became wealthy. The country gentleman's greatest satisfaction, however, lay in Lanquedoc's heightened position and power. Riquet died a year before the canal's opening in 1681 (a tradition repeated by Washington, who died just before the Pawtomack's opening, and by many later canal-builders whose deaths seemed synchronized with the completion of their canals), but he could already perceive the reinvigorated cities, the well-watered agriculture, the influx of outside wealth and foreign trade vessels. Most gratifying. In 1685, however, the Languedoc region broke out in a series of rebellions, religious, econmic, political, or all three.

As regional confidence increased and as Louis's persecutions intensified, Languedoc became the arena for bands of picturesque rebels who were called Camisards because of their colorful shirts (*camisa* being the Provençal word for "shirt"). Some historians identify these canal-region guerrillas as precursors of the rural activists of the French Revolution; the building of the canal thus appears to have played some role in the evolution of the French Republic.

Just as political consequences of the canal seem to have been revolutionary, its technological innovations were unprecedented. They were largely the achievement of Riquet's young and clever and not always respectful engineer, François Andréossy. The first task for the surveyors and engineers had been to locate a reliable water source to supply water for the canal at its 620-foot summit level. When they could not find any such natural source nearby, Andréossy and his colleagues determined to build one. They ordered construction of the massive earthen St. Féréol Dam, behind which mountain streams would fill a lake ample enough to feed the canal.

In order to build such a Cheops-worthy construction, Riquet had to conscript squads of peasant women from the region. During the course of the four arduous years of dam building, these women carried up on their shoulders an infinitude of baskets heaped high with earth; for each basketful they received a penny.

In other sections of the canal's construction, Riquet and Andréossy encountered the canal-builders' biggest frustration: soil that when mounded up for canal banks was not tight enough to retain the canal's water. The French engineers responded to the challenge of leaky earthen banks in the same way that English engineers did in the next century and American engineers did in yet the next—by commanding workers to "puddle" the soil. This is a process of turning and kneading the clayish earth again and again, much as a ceramicist blends oxygen with his clay and makes the mixture impermeable by turning and pummeling the materials.

There is a story of the Duke of Bridgewater's engineer James Brindley and puddling. As the much-honored engineer lay dying of exhaustion near a worksite, a frustrated foreman stormed into his residence, begging to know what to do about a bank that would not retain water.

"Puddle the soil," Brindley sighed.

The foreman explained that his workmen had already done so, repeatedly.

"Then puddle it again," Brindley said with his last breath.

Details of the construction of the Canal du Midi may not have been available to Elkanah Watson when he visited the site a century after completion. But he must have been particularly struck by the engineers' decision to build here (as in Briare) an independent artificial waterway up and over the watershed between the major rivers of the region. Rather than relying on the riverways and improving those unreliable streams, the builders ignored them and hung the canal on the walls of the flood-prone valleys. This was an important lesson for the Americans to learn.

To reach the man-made channel of the Canal du Midi, boats leave the Atlantic's Bay of Biscay behind them and pass through the Gironde Estuary to the Garonne River; soon they find themselves directed (near Langon) south and east in the direction of Toulouse. By means of 103 locks, the traffic, now as then, crosses the ridge and descends to the fantastic walled city of Carcassonne. From there the boats are conducted to the Mediterranean's Gulf of Lion near Narbonne. Although the Erie Canal, at 363 miles, is two and a half times longer than this route, the Canal du Midi rises more than 50 feet higher than the Erie's summit (at Buffalo)— nearly as high as the highest English canals built at the climax of the nineteenth century.

When Thomas Jefferson cruised down the "Languedoc Canal" two years before the French Revolution, he found it to be totally delightful as well as wondrously instructive. He marveled at the engineering, observed the industrious, awakened countryside, and pondered the relationship between such public works and government. These elaborate aqueducts,

these artful masonry locks, even these fountains in landscaped settings . . .
how might they be achieved by a democracy of confederated states? "I had
a great desire to examine [the situation] minutely," Jefferson wrote soon
after his May 1787 visit, "as at some future time it may enable me to give
information thereon to such of our states as are engaged in works of that
kind."

Take, for example, the very special locks that one finds here. Could
such handsome masonry constructions, built as well as anything of the
Romans, be afforded or risked by mere states? The locks had been designed in the form of curved chambers, both so that the curved sides of
oceangoing ships (as opposed to flat-sided canal barges) could be accepted
and so that the pressure of the surrounding water-heavy soils might be
resisted. No, the democratic state could most likely not afford or apply
these endless treasury outlays, these demanding imperial standards, and
these leisurely construction schedules (fifteen years were required for completion); nor could it command cooperative peasants to break their backs
for the king's pleasure.

Jefferson therefore concluded that for such lavish excellence in civic
design, some special "moral superiority" was needed. By this he meant a
rulership that was above the practicalities and responsibilities of small-
scaled democracies. Jefferson had in mind, presumably, a despot such as
the pharaoh who had ordered the construction of the first canal between
the Red Sea and the Mediterranean, or a lordly figure like Leonardo's
Duke of Milan. The price of such majesty and the public works that went
with it was undoubtedly too great, too punishing, for an American state
to contemplate.

Politics and Policies

Moral superiority in the mode of Louis XIV was not a distinguishing
feature of the United States government at this time of early canal-building—the time when Hamiltonian policies (no public debts) dominated.
Alexander Hamilton's wing of the Federalist Party had seized the reins of
power in the last decades of the eighteenth century. The Treasury Secretary's oft-heard dictum stated that neither the U.S. nor any other society
could succeed "which did not unite the interests and credit of rich individuals with those of the state." That attitude, which shunned high-rolling

schemes for public benefit, reigned without argument in contemporary ruling circles (as it does in many of today's ruling circles).

With this attitude dominant, the Federalist Party did all within its power to advance "internal improvements" (as canals and highways were called) not for the public or for regional advancement but for the united benefit of the rich landowners and the centralized government. Yet because of the limited means at their disposal and the primitive technology of the day, nothing greater than a turnpike here or a Patowmack Canal there resulted. The grand dreams of continental linkage that stirred George Washington and other Federalist leaders remained mere visions.

When Jefferson attained the White House and the "Jeffersonian Revolution" reached its apogee after 1801, the Democratic-Republicans were eager to do away with the internal-improvement programs initiated by previous regimes. Although the Jeffersonians recognized the need for improved transportation, they regarded it as essentially a state-by-state issue, certainly not something to be handled by a central bank for the benefit of private monopolies.

The Jeffersonians were no less eager to go West than the Federalists—particularly after Jefferson's Louisiana Purchase (1803). And in the opinion of historian Arthur M. Schlesinger, Jr., the Jeffersonians surrendered a number of their anticapitalist principles when they, perforce, allied themselves with local, state banks in order to finance transportation improvements. In many states, it could be said that the local banks owned the government.

At this time of economic change, the Jeffersonians continued to believe in an agricultural democracy and states' rights. Even though they subscribed to the emerging idea that a certain amount of industrialization was necessary (if only to support economic independence from Europe), they assumed that it could be localized. In the words of historical interpreters at the Lowell, Massachusetts, National Historic Park (where American industrialization began to happen), "Jefferson and his followers decided that the objectionable aspects of the European industrial experience could be avoided by the dispersal of manufacturing centers throughout the American countryside."

The most active proponent of the more conservative Jefferson philosophy was the talented Swiss-born Secretary of the Treasury, Albert Gallatin. His imaginative yet realistic *Report on Roads and Canals* (issued in

1808) set forth a wholly new program for dealing with the hugely expensive internal improvements that were now generally recognized as necessary for the states and the country. Believing that it was unrealistic as well as improper to call upon private capital for such undertakings—our few fortune-holders preferring to invest in land speculations or established businesses—he urged public-private cooperation. That is, he suggested that the federal government take responsibility for the internal improvements in cooperation with joint stock companies within the affected region.

By Gallatin's program (which anticipated but greatly differed from Henry Clay's better-known, more centralist "American System" of the 1820s), certain improvements were undertaken in continuation of the Federalists' undertakings. This was the time, for example, when a large federal grant was given for the development of the canal *parallel* to the Potomac River, the canal that later became the Chesapeake and Ohio. The Secretary's report had said that some $20 million was "available" for such projects. Jefferson himself, for all his belief in states' rights, had signed a bill in 1806 to commence work on the National Road through Maryland and Pennsylvania to the Ohio Valley.

For would-be canal-builders this news was tremendously exciting, if somewhat deceptive. Elkanah Watson was one of the most excited. He had in recent years focused his dreams on a trans–New York State canal, having moved to Albany after the Revolution and become a leading New York businessman. He had recently taken other New York leaders on a tour of the Mohawk Valley toward the Lake Ontario and Lake Erie to enlist those gentlemen in the canal-building cause. Now Watson assumed that in the Washington, D.C., of Albert Gallatin, money and energy could be found for a sea-to-lake canal.

When the New Yorkers, led by two notable legislators, Judge Joshua Gorman and William Kirkpatric, arrived in the capital to discuss their proposed canal with President Jefferson himself, they were received graciously but coolly. Jefferson's response:

It is a splendid project . . . and may be executed a century hence. Here [at the Potomac] is a canal of a few miles, projected by General Washington which has languished for many years because the small sum of $200,000 . . . [could not] be obtained. And you talk of making a canal three hundred and fifty miles long through a wilderness! It is little short of madness to think about it.

Evidently the Sage of Monticello had reached certain conclusions along the Languedoc Canal—conclusions about leadership, about financing, about the weaknesses of democratic states—that were deeply rooted: rustic, democratic Americans could not build grand canals. Nor were the Presidents who followed Jefferson any more positive.

When the War of 1812 burst upon the nation, with its disruption of commerce and its destruction of whatever financial surplus the nation may have acquired, it appeared impossible for canal-makers, in New York or elsewhere, to expect the desired funding from Washington. President Madison, when confronted with the issue, was rather pallidly in favor of internal improvements but suspected that they posed constitutional problems.

Much as the Jeffersonians may have yearned for certain internal improvements, political philosophy and much more prevented them from taking action. Like the Federalists, post-1801 administrations were prevented from building the routes West by lack of capital, lack of a mass labor pool or of advanced technology, and lack of geologists and engineers (though some engineers now began to come forth from West Point). The contorted mountains that blocked the way West were perhaps the most difficult problem. Not until we paid attention to our own land and understood its peculiarities could we learn how to work westward across it.

The Puzzle of the Appalachians

Fold after fold of Appalachian ridges strike the eye as one flies south and west over the region today. They bear local names: the Catskills, the Poconos, the Blue Ridge, the Shenandoahs. And ultimately the westward flier faces the Allegheny Front, as it's called, the escarpment beyond which lies the Appalachian Plateau; it stretches from Georgia to Lake Erie. The trip West would crack any axle, break the back of any mule . . . unless a waterway could be woven around and between the summits.

And in this geographical chaos, how could a canal-builder armed only with a compass figure out the precise gradients for his watercourse? Among these Appalachian mountain ranges, many critical passes demanded that the route ascend to 2,000 feet, as opposed to 600 feet for England's Pennine chain. And the distance the ditch would have to traverse, from eastern commencement point to western terminus, would be in the hundreds rather than the scores of miles, mostly through uncharted, unpopulated wilderness.

There were, to be sure, surveyors who, like George Washington, had sufficient skills to compute distances and to lay out preferable routes through the Appalachians. Yet to chart exact differences in elevation was a challenge that continued to lie beyond their capacities. Also, to work with, dig at, blast away all these rocks and stumps in any efficient manner was beyond the knowledge of contemporary contractors. The Appalachians rose to their heights mysterious, unknowable, impenetrable, a region for native hunters, wretched pioneers, outcast traders.

But the eighteenth century was the Age of Enlightenment, urging upon man bold confidence in his ability to explore and understand the world around him; he would, obeying the instruction in Genesis, "take dominion" of it. Elkanah Watson had apparently concluded, as he studied the Mohawk Valley and the way to Lake Erie, that he had come upon a unique continental opportunity: the one and only broad passageway westward to the Allegheny Plateau and the Great Lakes. There were, of course, some gaps to the south—the Cumberland Gap, where a turnpike ran, and the twisty path through the hills of Maryland and what later became West Virginia, where General Braddock had built his road in the French and Indian Wars. But these were more trouble than they were worth, in Watson's opinion. Here in New York State there was a broad, wide-open route that could only be compared to the even broader valley between France's Pyrenees and Central Massif; the natural route to the unification of the nation's Atlantic and its interior seas lay before him.

To the north of the proposed New York route were the Adirondacks, to the south the Catskills. The Mohawk led directly to Oneida Lake—which rested at virtually the same elevation as Lake Ontario, only 25 miles away. Furthermore, if canal-builders were to follow the "Genesee Turnpike" toward the west from the shores of Lake Oneida, they would have no serious ascent problem until the very end of the route. There one encountered the Niagara Escarpment, a barrier to be surmounted before a boat could reach Lake Erie. The argument was hard to counter that this was indeed a divinely created pathway.

In our own, scientific age we expect geology to explain neatly and logically what happened to the earth here—yet geologists admit that much mystery remains. Certainly the Appalachians and their formation have been an elusive subject for generations. Science writer John McPhee reports that the puzzle of these mountains' origins was totally beyond the scope of our first naturalists; for many years solving it remained the "prime object" of American geologists. And they are still trying.

By the professionals we are urged to think in terms of "orogenic cycles"—different earth spasms forming different ranges. Ever since the 1960s, when the theories of the German geologist Alfred Wegener became generally accepted, we have been encouraged to comprehend the dynamics of plate tectonics. Huge, inchoate protocontinents are visualized as sliding out of control across the globe and crashing into each other. The language is quite wonderful: we feel engaged in the gods' game of "continental drift." Poor Elkanah Watson knew nothing about this as he strove to understand the Mohawk Valley.

It appears that the oldest of the Appalachian accidents, the "Avalonian Orogeny," occurred some 570 million years ago. It was this disruption that brought forth the ancient mountains of New England. Then, 440 million years ago, when the landmass that would become eastern Canada ("Laurentia") banged into northern Europe ("Baltica"), there occurred the "Taconian Orogeny," which created the Adirondacks. Some 150 million years later, North America suffered a midsection assault by Africa, causing the "Alleghenian Orogeny." This monumental collision reverberated for fifty million years, as volcanoes erupted and jagged peaks (including the Catskills) rose higher and higher against the reddened skies, reaching the elevation of today's Himalayas.

Greatly eroded, the Appalachians now slumber upon their bases. Yet although they look from the air like one simultaneously wrought chain, we are to remember that each link, each range, was forged individually, in its own time of fire. Also, because the eastern part of North America spent so much of its early life in contact with parts of Europe and Africa, we should recognize that we share with those continents a number of *mutual* rock formations. Further, because these cataclysmic events took place when these continental bits and pieces were near the equator (and when the earth was warmer), tropical swamps grew where now we see snow-topped ridges—with the result that in the pressure-tight seams of these ridges, both here and in Europe, early prospectors found the coal that had once been lush vegetation. It was for the transportation of this coal, the basic fuel of the industrial revolution, that many of the canals were built. Thus does orogeny press upon human affairs.

But suddenly, science magazines proclaim, the plate tectonics theory is out the window; the situation is far more complex than we'd been advised. No longer viewed as totally authoritative are such spokesmen for continental drift as J. Tuzo Wilson of *Ontario Science*—who used to write about how "bits of Georgia were left in Africa; pieces of Europe stuck to Canada and New England." Now a generation of scientists posits that there were many, many more bits and pieces crashing around than Dr. Wilson ever imagined, over a far longer period of time.

For all who would understand the unique route of the Erie Canal, beginning with the Mohawk Valley's passageway through the mountains, it would also be helpful to have an explanation for the phenomenon of the Hudson River Valley. This dramatic passageway gave the New York State canal-planners their essential link with the Atlantic. The Hudson's north-south bed may represent, the tectonicists used to tell us, an ages-old rift line between two of the proto continents (just as the Mohawk Valley may represent a neutral zone between two orogenies). Another theory is that rift or fault lines may have something to do with the rotation of the earth around its axis: the spinning causes such physical strain that the earth's surface develops abysmal cracks.

Before geology attempted to figure out these things, divine intent was credited as sufficient explanation for both of these God-given routes. But one would also have to wonder why the Almighty made things so very difficult for the boatman who would go north on the Hudson and west on the Mohawk. Slightly upriver from Albany, the early boatman had to leave the Hudson and attempt to pole, push, or drag his light craft up and around the 200-foot-high rock face or raging Cohoes Falls to the superior level of the Mohawk. Then he would have to ascend another 200 feet— including a conquest of the dangerous rapids at Little Falls—before arriving at the Oneida Lake level. This was indeed a splendid and unique route, but it was as challenging to traverse as it was to understand.

Looking forward rather than backward into time, it must also have been difficult for the frustrated boatman or for the ambitious Elkanah

Watson to understand how or when our own canal-builders could improve this first part of the waterway so that it could carry freight- or passenger-burdened vessels to the Great Lakes. But gradually, as Americans focused on the rich possibilities of their westward land and collected rumors and reports about the canals of Europe, they seemed to swell with an optimism worthy of superman. Astonishing reports of canal developments—not only in England but also on our own shores—added to fantasies of accomplishment.

Early Canals and Contraptions

By 1790, more than thirty canal corporations had been founded in eight of the original thirteen states. These hopeful societies, concentrated on local improvements, were all more or less contemporaries of George Washington's Patowmack Company. Most often their achievements were rather primitive, imitative locks around river blockages. But occasionally they were more than that, more natively ingenious, more nationally promising.

There was, for example, the impressive Santee-Cooper Canal in South Carolina. This 22-mile lateral canal, connecting two rivers that traversed the same coastal plain, was chartered in 1786 and completed in 1800. But for two facts, it might be argued that this was the earliest significant American canal. First, the canal was constructed by slaves at the orders and for the private benefit of certain plantation owners who wished to ship their own agricultural products from the interior to the port of Charleston; it did not exist for the transportation of other people's commercial goods or for the public at large. Second, the brains behind the construction belonged not to an inventive southerner but to an irascible Swede, John Christian Senf. This canal worked splendidly and profitably when many others did not.

Nonetheless, it was not the plantation owners of the South but the would-be industrial lords of the North who initially accepted the challenge of taking Americans West by canal. That is clearly the opinion of canal historian Henry Sinclair Drago, who wrote: "Public interest in a man-made waterway was first displayed in New England." The relationship between that public interest and private gain is a subtle matter. Is it in the interest of the public to be directed by the dictates of a new industrial system? Possibly.

In the eyes of contemporary New Englanders, there seemed to be two ways of reaching the interior—that is, two ways to tap the resources of *their* West (which was, actually, the rich timberland and potentially productive area of New Hampshire and Vermont). One way, eagerly eyed by the merchants of Boston, was the Merrimack River, which had the virtue of easy access to the north and west but also the regrettable flaw of reaching the sea not at Boston but farther north, near Newburyport. The other way, eyed with equal covetousness by Connecticut Yankees dwelling along Long Island Sound, was the Connecticut River. It went straight as an arrow into the interior, but was impeded by many falls and rapids in the course of its passage. One or another of these ways, promoted by enthusiasts of that region, would provide America with its first public canal, America's first route West by water.

The eventual success of the Bostonians—who called their waterway the Middlesex Canal, because it went from Boston Harbor to Middlesex Village on the Merrimack River—was recognized by leaders of the day as the great victory that it was. Chartered in 1793 and completed in 1803, the 27-mile-long construction was called by Albert Gallatin "the greatest work of [its] kind which has been completed in the United States."

But even as the Boston canal-planners secured their charter and got themselves organized, news came of alarming developments along the Connecticut: their rivals there had already obtained a charter under the name "Company for Rendering the Connecticut River Navigable." Their program called for a canal of nine locks that would bypass the 42-foot cataract at Bellows Falls. Financed by Englishmen (two brothers from London named Atkinson), the bypass canal would be accompanied by other improvements that would make the river navigable for 120 miles above the entrepôt at Walpole, New Hampshire. The Boston merchants, while threatened by this development, may have contented themselves with the fact that reaching Walpole from the interior wasn't quite the same thing as reaching the sea.

Soon came reports of an even more audacious undertaking farther down the Connecticut River: a strange-sounding lift device called the "Hampshire Machine" had been put into operation at South Hadley,

33

Massachusetts, its purpose being to get boats up and over the falls. This project was twinned with an effort to build a bypass canal some miles upriver at Turners Falls. The combined maneuver had been initiated by a zealous group of Connecticut Yankees who had moved upriver from New Haven to South Hadley in the 1780s; they sought to fulfill the objectives of the "Proprietors of the Locks and Canals on the Connecticut River," appointed by the state's general court. The operation was well organized, with an expected completion date of 1792.

In an effort to make up for the regions's lack of engineering expertise, a consultant from New York had been brought in to help the locals, and a clever Yankee mechanic named Benjamin Prescott was found in Northampton to mastermind the work. His main predicament was how to surmount the 50-foot-high red sandstone bluff at South Hadley and to afford passage to the river level beyond. The Hampshire Machine was his solution—a response that should be hailed for its technological ingenuity even as we chuckle at its primitive giganticism. Described some years after its installation by Yale's far-traveling president Timothy Dwight, the machine consisted of a mighty waterwheel-powered axle that turned two "spur wheels" 20 feet in diameter. These, in turn, served to wind up the chains which hauled a boat-carrying cart up out of a lock and along an inclined plane to a lock chamber fed by the damned river at the higher end.

The complexity of the contraption must have been hard to believe in that simple, rural scene. The inclined plane was 230 feet long and built of stone covered by heavy planking. The cart had three sets of wheels, the second and third progressively larger than the first so the cart could remain level as it ascended the 13½-degree slope. The lower lock had to be literally carved out of the sandstone by a force of 250 men, as the rock was considered to be too hard for pick and shovel and too dangerously soft for blasting powder. Yet the work was accomplished on schedule, at the staggering cost of $81,375.

34   By the summertime of 1795, northbound riverboats, each carrying as much as 7,000 pounds of freight (usually hardware to be traded for agricultural and forest products from New Hampshire and Vermont), were arriving in great numbers before the lock gates at the bottom of the system. After a boat had entered the lock and settled into the cradle upon the car, the Hampshire machine would start to grind the wheeled vehicle up the inclined plane to the upper chamber. The upward ride took but six minutes. Then the boat would be towed out of the lock by oxen and driver, the whole process having been accomplished in little more than a quarter of an hour. And it cost the shipper only four shillings, sixpence—something like 75 cents—for each ton of freight transported over the falls.

Yankees evidently had both the will and the ingenuity to take the lead in canal pioneering. In New England there seemed to be both a mechanically adept work force and effective planners. They would make the most of their land. South Hadley provided a clue to why New England became the laboratory in which talented locals would make small-scale experiments for the later larger-scale benefit of the entire nation.

But as Bostonians and other skeptics looked more closely at the South Hadley experiment, there also seemed to be some inherent difficulties, negative features that boded ill for similar systems elsewhere. First and foremost, the cost, while not beyond reason, had been too steep for local investors; Dutch financiers had been invited to bear most of the strain (just as English investors had been called upon at Bellows Falls). Perhaps even the ambitious Yankees could not afford to pay their own way into the industrial age. Second, there were technical and economic consequences from this river improvement which were unfortunate. Not only were the cables snapping and the operational costs mounting higher than predicted, but also local farmers and fishermen were condemning the project because of both flooding and the smell of stagnant water behind the dam.

The dam was, in fact, disrupting the fragile local economy *for the benefit of the owners of the facility*—who were realizing something like $12,000 in tolls a year, enough to pay back the Dutchmen. Complaints multiplied, becoming a roar of lower-class rage. If Thomas Jefferson had been acquainted with this incendiary situation, he would undoubtedly have smiled. In a democracy, what petty annoyances can be caused by the likes of farmers and fishermen! Only in an empire or monarchy could a superior leader wave his scepter and accomplish such a glorious thing as a canal, perfectly executed and beyond question.

But in South Hadley things eventually worked themselves out. The complaints of the citizenry were listened to and acted upon; money for improvements was squeezed out of the local skinflints. To combat the fever and agues brought on by the stagnant water, a giant lottery was staged for a war chest. Some $2,000 was raised to lower the dam and to meet other demands. Democracy seemed capable of rising to vigorous challenge.

By 1805, the wondrous Hampshire Machine had been replaced by a more modern series of double-gated locks. The early experiment gave way to more standardized, trouble-free solutions to the problem. Traffic flowed, and the new Canal Village at the base of the falls flourished. Boston, where financiers were still getting themselves organized to harness the Merrimack, got the message that unless fast action was taken, access to the riches north and west would belong exclusively to the Connecticut Yankees.

New England's Premier Canal

This business of local canals undoubtedly sounds petty and far removed from the grand patterns of national destiny. But, as noted by that precocious observer J. Hector St. John Crèvecoeur, in America "all is local"; that's what our history is fundamentally about. In New England, as the eighteenth century ended—and fear intensified that the once-mighty fortune-producing overseas trade in tall ships was failing—rivalry for control of the interior became even more acute. Boston industrialists reacted in alarm to the news that certain merchant kings in Newburyport were planning to overcome the difficulties of the Merrimack River and direct traffic from west and north to their port city. Swift steps would have to be taken to overcome or outflank their waterway. Newburyport, indeed!

These adventurers called themselves the "Proprietors of Locks and Canals on the Merrimack River," and while Boston dozed they had managed to obtain one of the first corporate charters granted in the United States. They authorized the commencement of work at the formidable Pawtucket Falls (near present-day Lowell) in 1792. And their proposition seemed quite reasonable: why should they as possessors of the river's mouth not expect to see, after river improvements modeled along the lines of successes elsewhere, a sudden boom of traffic and a great flood of raw materials, all streaming through their prospering city?

Despite the growing strengths of Jefferson's Democrat-Republicans elsewhere, these rival New England canal-builders, including the financiers who at length triumphed with their Merrimack Canal, remained staunch Federalists. In New England there were some Jeffersonians, but they were farmers and "mechanics." The latter term referred to artisans and laborers who had found employment within the region's few existing industries. The ancient aristocracy that the Federalist Party represented in New England remained strong, rich, and powerfully determined that they and their families would be the ones who would benefit primarily if any internal improvements were made and new industries developed. Ownership of the land gave them that eternal right, as they saw it.

The hugely dominant signature of John Hancock had symbolized daring patriotism when seen on the Declaration of Independence. But when seen on the initial prospectus of the proprietors of the Middlesex Canal (dated September 2, 1793), it symbolized a different spirit—a kind of antidemocratic arrogance.

Hancock and his confederates by no means shared the Jeffersonians' fear of private monopolies taking over and owning a state's internal improvements. Their view of social morality differed but little from the old model in England. In the Federalist era, neither full votes nor adequate pay could be expected by the common man, least of all an equal chance at a better life. Yet it's also notable that John Hancock signed this key document in the next-to-last month of his life; his order was on its way out. The canal that he and his fellow proprietors financed played an unintended role in that socioeconomic shift.

The magnificence of the Federalist order still glowed brightly in 1793, however. Distinguished officers in the Revolution and now prominent merchants or statesmen, these proprietors of the Middlesex Canal had every reason to regard themselves as the perpetual lords of the Commonwealth. Included among them was wealthy Christopher Gore of Waltham, whose brick mansion of bas-relief arches and subtle pilasters still seduces viewers into wondering what could possibly be wrong with wealth so beautiful.

President of the board was General (later Governor) James Sullivan, whose brother John, by his slaughters among the Iroquois in 1779, happened to have cleared out of the way all Indians who might have objected

37

to the building of the Erie Canal on their land. Fortunately for the Middlesex, the hard-driving and self-seeking James Sullivan was as sincerely interested in the creation of the public canal as he was in improving his personal fortune. An associate wrote of him: "His mind was not only uncommonly comprehensive, but always on the stretch."

In terms of getting the Middlesex Canal built and solving its fundamental problems, the most significant individual was Colonel Loammi Baldwin. Sheriff of Middlesex County, Baldwin had been trained as a cabinetmaker and also had a reputation as a specialist in pumps and hydraulics. Of mechanical bent, his mind was inventive if not intellectual. Early in his life, before the Revolution, he had attended scientific lectures presented by Professor John Winthrop at Harvard (which university Baldwin did *not* attend as a formal student, despite the claim of some biographies). At those lectures he befriended another sit-in student, the Tory-inclined Benjamin Thompson, who, as "Count Rumford," gained fame for inventing the marine steam engine after fleeing to England. This was a century for minds of such originality and divergence.

Baldwin's popular renown, ironically, stems not so much from his contributions to the technology of America's industrial revolution as from his association with that faithful agricultural product the Baldwin apple. According to Mary Stetson Clarke's lively book on the Middlesex Canal, the first surveying party for the canal's route came upon the sight of numerous woodpeckers enjoying the tart, juicy apples of a particular tree in the wild. Hearing of this, Baldwin took cuttings from the tree and planted them on his estate. Soon the young trees were yielding fruit that became a major product of the region, shipped down the canal from Baldwin's orchards to markets in Boston.

Marketer and inventor, Baldwin had to become a diplomat as well to attract the key person to plan and design a canal that was truly beyond the capacities of the region's "ingenious" Yankees. For it was recognized that nowhere in New England or all the United States was there an engineer who could manage the precise topographical measurements that would allow a summit-level canal to be built, specifically the proposed canal between the Merrimack River and Boston's Charles River Basin. The proprietors nearly despaired of finding a way to correct the woefully inaccurate first measurements for the suggested route. Then, hearing reports that the distinguished canal-builder William Weston (protégé of the

Duke of Bridgewater's engineer James Brindley) was to be found in the United States at that moment, the proprietors appointed Baldwin to go to Philadelphia and some how or other lure the diffident Englishman to Boston in order to make an accurate survey of the canal route. Along the way, Weston was expected to suggest solutions to any significant engineering problems encountered in the field.

On arriving at the nation's then capital, Loammi Baldwin soon understood the lay of the land: William Weston was totally devoted to unraveling the engineering problems of the Schuylkill-Susquehanna and Schuylkill-Delaware canals (which were to have troubled existences, beginning in the year of their creation, 1794; see Chapter 5). Baldwin understood, on the other hand, that Mrs. Weston, for her part, seemed more interested in American society than in American canals; she seemed particularly interested in whatever she could learn about Boston society. Baldwin's letters home noted that the Englishwoman, having learned as much as she could about how American society worked, "observed that all the English Gentlemen and Ladies enjoyed themselves better in Boston than any place on [this] continent." So, Baldwin thought, might she not be persuaded to lead her husband in a northeasterly direction?

The Westons were finally induced to make the journey to the Puritan capital in the summer of 1794. One must trust that Mrs. Weston was not disappointed. Weston brought with him to Boston a precious instrument, the "Wye level," composed of magnetic needle, spirit level, and telescope—a seemingly magical device, never before seen here—and with it succeeded in eliminating previous discrepancies in the Middlesex Canal's route surveys. William Weston's work was expert, dilligent, and far-reaching. His projections for the locks, bridges, culverts, and aqueducts for the canal were immensely helpful (though he did not, in fact, *build* the canal). Now the work could go forward with confidence.

As well as helping Philadelphia's and Boston's would-be canal-builders, William Weston also assisted the canal-builders along the Potomac. He was invited to travel down to that difficult river in 1795, having been requested by the President to deliver a critique on the locks then being constructed at Great Falls. But if George Washington had hoped that the English engineer would solve the canal's problems, he was to be severely disappointed. Weston made helpful remarks but could do nothing about a canal situated in the bed of a river that flooded so frequently.

39

Another traveler to the Potomac who denigrated its improvements at this time was Loammi Baldwin; he went down to see exactly how those heavily endowed locks and slave-carved cuts actually worked. (This was many years before the Jefferson-era decision to construct a man-made channel that would parallel the Potomac.) "I have never seen one foot of Canal which has been completed in a proper and the most approved manner," Baldwin wrote. Also he warned the proprietors, "I have been in several public works of this kind (though inferior), yet I never knew any but what had Periods of difficulty and required the aid an attention of the whole." He chose his words of warning with care.

Baldwin may have sounded modest and self-effacing in his report on the Potomac, but this conscientious, pragmatic apple-grower was just what the Middlesex Canal needed. For this canal, though charted by Weston's experienced eye, became the hand-crafted creation of Loammi Baldwin; he put everything he had into it, expecting that both he and his region would flourish as a result of the work. Somehow the massive wooden house that now stands on the banks of a restored section of the canal in Woburn, Massachusetts, the town in which the Baldwin family had lived for generations, seems a true, monumental representation of the individual.

A handsome, if somewhat flaking, example of late Georgian/early Federalist architecture, with heavy window casements, ponderous quoins, and wood-block facing, the mansion provides a splendid stage setting for this drama of regional paternalism. Baldwin's "Homestead" has been moved in recent times to a site not far from its original location; yet one can easily see it as it originally functioned, surrounded by gardens and orchards, indentured servants at their tasks, the canal flowing across the foot of the 150 acres. Perhaps this rustic neoclassical mansion was no match for the elegant chateau of Pierre Paul Riquet, father of the Canal du Midi, but it loomed equally large on the landscape as proper home for the regional hero.

40

Dump Carts on the Middlesex

At the moment when the first shovel dug the first divot for the canal (September 10, 1794), Loammi Baldwin delivered the official invocation.

He prayed that "the Eye of Wisdom and the Eternal Mind aid this work, designed for the benefit of the present and all Future Generations." This bizarre theological language reflects the fact that Baldwin, like George Washington and most of the Federalist leadership, was a Deist, believing not in the traditional Christian, three-person God but in a kind of grand engineer of the universe.

Some serious legal and financial work by mortals had to be completed, however, before the Eye of Wisdom could oversee the construction. By persuasion and purchase and hornswoggling, the proprietors sought to acquire acreage along the route of the canal. Some of the citizens, caught up in the spirit of the "public" endeavor, gladly contributed requested parcels. And some accepted without grumbling the sales price offered by the canal corporation. But others (particularly those who feared floods, muskrats, and get-rich-quick Federalists) were obdurate in their refusal to sell. Why should they help John Hancock make yet another fortune? So, for the first time in the history of the Commonwealth of Massachusetts, the power of eminent domain was unleashed. Soon the entire route from Boston to Middlesex Village (now a part of Lowell) fell into the hands of the corporation, 142 individual parcels of land.

The next question was who (under the direction of the eternal Eye of Wisdom) would do the physical work. Some of the digging was contracted out to established companies in New Hampshire and Massachusetts, but the bulk of the work was taken on by farmer-landowners in localities along the 27-mile route. Each of these contractors—paid greater or lesser amounts depending on the difficulty of the terrain—found kinsmen and neighbors who had shovels and might be able to spare a day or two from field and barnyard to help with the digging.

Excavation of the canal bed began at the western shore of the millpond formed by the Concord River at Billerica. Then and there was established the tradition among American canal builders that the ditch be started at a spot that seemed most politically advisable, most attention-getting, and most likely to facilitate progress. The surveys of William Weston had indicated that this Billerica millpond lay at the summit level of the projected canal; anything from here would be downhill, either way.

The millpond reflected sun and clouds at an altitude of 107.99 feet above sea level at Boston harbor. Toward the west (ah, the West!) the canal was to descend 27 feet, by means of three locks, to the Merrimack River, less than 6 miles away. Toward the east (that is, from the eastern side of the pond), the canal was to step down 100 feet by means of thirteen locks to the Charles River, 22 miles distant. As well as those sixteen locks (plus two more at the entrances, for a total of twenty locks) there would be eight aqueducts over the streams and rivers that ran north and south across the way.

Among Weston's more imaginative concepts for the canal was that Billerica Pond was to be spanned by a *floating* towpath. Until this point, the towpath stretched along the 10-foot-wide top of the canal's higher bank (the other side, the "berm" or "heelpath" side, was only 5 feet wide at its top). Arriving at the millpond, the tow boy and his horses would step out onto a pontoon-supported plankway that allowed them to keep going across the center of the water surface. Being a millpond, it was usually serene.

Of course, there were such difficulties as berm walls that simply did not seem capable of holding water. And Baldwin (who earned the nickname "America's James Brindley" for resembling that Briton in his unflagging attention to construction details) was always there when workmen needed his attention to any such plaguing problem. For tools the men and boys had nothing but shovels, pickaxes, and carts—tools that we today would consider utterly inadequate for such a large-scale project. Yet they puddled and repuddled the rocky, intractable soils of the leaking sections. Finally Baldwin invented a way of ram-pounding the soil that seemed to be effective in this part of the geologically mysterious world. In the New England way, they "made do" with what they had.

Loammi Baldwin also made an improvement on the traditional earth-carrying cart, inventing a way to swing it up on its axle and dump it— ancestor of the dump truck. The iron parts of mallets and other tools were forged in the canal corporation's blacksmith shop in Billerica. Wood shafts for ax and pick handles were turned out at the corporation's sawmill. Aided by these trustworthy products and pressed by Baldwin's unflagging zeal, the contractors and workmen moved ahead, a shovelful at a time, every day but Sunday, season after season.

The hope of finishing the work in a couple of years faded. Baldwin's frustrations at various delays were magnified by pressures from the pro-

42

prietors and directors, including confused commands and binding restric-
tions. With the ultimate howl of a harassed executive, he wrote in January
1798, ". . . it is inconceivable how much such things [as fouled-up com-
munications] embarrass. Waiting for orders, expecting or realizing a change
in the arrangements or operations confounds, obstructs, and defeats."
Then Baldwin reached the point where the whole business seemed too
much to bear; he wrote in his diary in March 1803 that he was "pretty
much determined to quit the canal."

James Sullivan and the other officers urged him to reconsider. "Let
me, therefore . . . beseech you . . ." Sullivan wrote him. Gradually little
celebrations were held to mark points at which the canal work had been
completed; water was allowed to flow from point to point, and the increased number of cheering voices helped Baldwin believe that the whole
system could be made to work. He himself gave a "moderate collation and
Treat" when the Middlesex Canal Company completed a gristmill and
sawmill in the newly thriving community that had sprung up at the millpond on the Concord River.

But before the official celebrations could be held to mark the canal's
entire completion (which occurred on the last day of 1803), the numerous
locks and adqueducts had to be given their finishing touches and then
tested. Remembering the advice on these matters given by Weston, yet
pressed by his superiors to cut costs and get the cursed canal finished so
the revenues could flow, Baldwin occasionally resorted to homemade
innovations. Although he had heard about Brindley's massive, vault-sup-
ported masonry aqueducts, he also had a certain trust in wooden troughs
that he (as a former cabinetmaker) was sure would hold water adequately.
So, when called to span the distance between the abutments of a projected
aqueduct, he hammered together a rough-board trough, then built enough
stone piers (resting on the riverbed below) to hold up the box plus the
water that would fill it. By this technique, Baldwin and his workers devised
aqueducts more expeditious than permanent.

Today a traveler along the old canal's unwatered course can see the
still-impressive remains of the aqueduct Baldwin built across the Shawsheen River. And one can sight through the U-shaped notch in the abutment at one end to the notches in the central pier and in the abutment
beyond, to see how the wooden trough was set into its stone supports.

When first built, however, the river was wider and the abutments farther apart; two additional piers had been necessary to span the total distance of 188 feet. The trough carried the canal water at a height more than 30 feet above the river's surface—quite an accomplishment for an era of hammers and shovels.

The locks that Baldwin attempted to build out of wood were less successful, constantly needing repair and replacement. He had to confess to his diary on October 18, 1796, that the very first locks he and a noted contractor had built in Middlesex Village collapsed at their first trial: "Opened Lock and Canal at Merrimack River and the first Lock Broak and failed." Nonetheless, he retained confidence that local stonemasons could swiftly set the situation right; better that, he thought, than invest the company's dwindling funds in the expensive brickwork constructions proposed by Weston. Sure enough, on the second attempt the new stone lock at Middlesex Village functioned perfectly.

A year later, however, when the directors of the canal were celebrating the near-completion of the first section by building two canalboats for a voyage down from Billerica Pond to the Merrimack, Baldwin had to express some reservations about certain weak points that might give way. Brushing his fears aside, the directors went ahead with their festive celebration, proceeding in their boats merrily down the staircase of locks from the Concord River. Baldwin then suffered the mortification of watching as the wall of one of the three locks at Middlesex Village gave way when the boats passed through. Nothing daunted, the directors continued on their way to a nearby tavern, happy to authorize that the workmen who had assisted their expedition be treated to a meal of 150 pounds of roast beef, two bushels of potatoes, and an entire barrel of cider. Despite a few forgettable details, the voyage had to be hailed as a triumph.

Loammi Baldwin was able to take deserved pride in another aspect of the work. He noted that upon the opening of this westernmost section of the canal, the most critical feature of the system's construction—the water level and flow—worked precisely as planned. Specifications had called for a water surface that would be 30½ feet wide between banks, and a water-way that would be virtually level between the west end of Billerica Pond and the first of the three locks leading down to the Merrimack. Baldwin commented with satisfaction at the time of the directors' celebratory voyage: "The *level* by which the work was executed from the Concord River to the Merrimack, about five and three-quarter miles, proves exact. I cannot perceive by the water that it varies one quarter of an inch." Cider was indeed called for all around.

But as the project dragged on from 1791 into the opening years of the new century, increasing amounts of money were needed. The directors tried public lotteries to bring in extra funds, with only partial success. Weary stockholders were assessed an additional $10 a share in 1794—a continuing draw upon their purses that became a local tradition. By 1817, for those who cared to count them, there had been one hundred further assessments, as improvements continued to be necessary after completion.

James Sullivan's major function as president was to entertain and reassure the proprietors and stockholders—a public relations role to which he devoted himself with unrestrained gusto. As a result of his festivals, boat trips, and excursions with enthusiasts, he persuaded the stockholders to keep coming up with the needed funds. They felt a certain suspicious euphoria as their stock's value rose from $25 a share in 1794 to $473 at the year of completion (1803) and to $500 the year after that, but still more money was needed. Was the canal a success or not?

The directors, also suspicious, commanded Baldwin to cut all costs in the final years of construction. Though the decision had been made to build the most important locks in stone—and the best stone for the lock sills and sides was expensive New Hampshire granite—the new order forced a return to wood. So it happened that at the critical point in the eastern section, Stoddard's Locks, where the waterway descended 50 feet through three sets of double chambers, the locks had to built of wood. Baldwin (and, from afar, Weston) protested that this would simply mean more expense later on. But the directors insisted on getting the job done, starting up the revenue stream, and leaving future problems to the future.

Wherever possible, Baldwin used his own ingenuity—and his forceful personality—to achieve quality work, even while going along with the directors' pinch-penny edicts. There's the story, for example, of his need to locate a proper hydraulic cement. This material was essential to the underwater security of the locks: mortar to seal the joints of the locks had to be found or the constructions would leak and eventually buckle. Many European lock builders had used "trass" for this purpose, volcanic mud

45

collected from along the Rhine River; others (including the Romans) had used a volcanic ash found at the base of Mount Vesuvius. In his survey of the Middlesex Canal route, Weston spotted some likely-looking material within hauling distance from the canal. But Baldwin's experiments, mixing the material with ashes and lime, proved disappointing. What was America's first native-born canal engineer to do about this fundamental deficiency?

He had heard that volcanic material much like trass was to be found on the Dutch island of St. Eustatius in the West Indies, well within the range of Yankee merchant ships. So he called together the board of directors and, to their loud complaints, declared it absolutely necessary for a shipment of the material to be obtained, at once. He explained logically that money had to be spent on this quest then or the locks would never be watertight. The directors finally agreed; a trading vessel with an outward-bound cargo of lumber was instructed to stop off at St. Eustatius and negotiate. The international business having been transacted, Baldwin got his precious cargo. And when he found that mixing the trass in the approved European manner was too time-consuming and expensive, he invented a way of grinding the foreign ash first before mixing it with lime. The resultant cement was effective and relatively inexpensive.

Baldwin is also remembered for his invention of a horse-powered "water machine." Always a pump expert, he constructed this device to keep water out of a lock chamber when in construction. Pacing on a treadmill, a horse drove the shaft of a massive-capacity water-exhaust system. It worked; the long-delayed, much-contested locks were finished.

Finally, on the last day of December in 1803, the canal was declared completed, hailed by general celebrations. Loammi Baldwin, though exhausted and dissatisfied with some of the work, agreed that the project and his part in it had come to an acceptable end; he had certainly earned his fee of $1,000 a year.

His canal had cost $528,000—an almost unheard-of expenditure in those days of minute capitalization. It was an investment made by individual entrepreneurs (as opposed to the later Erie Canal's financing, which was largely by local banks), wealthy gentlemen who believed in a richer future for themselves and their city. By this investment, they would become factors in the increased shipping of goods to market and in the oncoming industrialization of the region. Much of their dream came true: Boston, having tapped the resources of its northwestern interior, had its moment in the sun as a leading center of U.S. commerce.

The Social and Industrial Awakening

Even as tolls began to flow into the company from the brisk traffic east and west, and as two stations were installed for the precise measurement of freightage, skeptics continued to doubt the canal's financial viability. The income was definitely healthy: the 6¼ cents charged per mile for every ton of freight began to produce revenues in the thousands during the earliest years of operations, and by the 1820s, commercial traffic was so heavy that $20,000 a year was coming into the canal company. By that time, according to the treasurer, meticulous Charles Francis Adams, the carrying of goods to and from the new factories at Lowell contributed more than a third of the total receipts. The canal had begun its life for the transport of agricultural and forest products (plus stone) but had gone on to become a medium for the new industrialism.

But expenses of maintenance and replacement increased along with the tolls. One had to look at a multidimensional balance sheet, weighing both specific and peripheral benefits, present and potential income, against the costs. From the point of view of the riders, for example, there was no doubt whatsoever about the economic success of the enterprise. For a mere 75 cents, passengers could float the whole way from Boston to Lowell, enjoying an outing that became known as the cheapest and most popular mode of public transportation in the East.

These early American canalboat riders were surprised and delighted to find the experience far more comfortable than the bouncing and jouncing of land travel. The sensation of "gliding along a silver ribbon of water" (in words of a later time) made travel not a burden but a pleasure.

From the departure point at Charlestown, the company's boats left each morning for Middlesex Village. Though the trip was leisurely, since laws to protect the banks against wake wash restricted boat speed to 4 miles an hour, it had its thrills. There were the locks, such as those that carried the canal up and over the Mystic River—allowing the passengers to sample the ciders and viands at nearby taverns. And there were the

47

sights, the beautiful, winding passageway through low hills to the Mystic Lakes and to Horn Pond. Before that pond there was the excitement of the considerable climb at Stoddard's Locks, followed by the ride up through Woburn and North Woburn (with a few glimpses of Loammi Baldwin's mansion). Then there was the famous "Oxbow Curve" in today's Wilmington Town Forest, where the embankments swung the canal clear of a swamp by means of a tight curve.

Ultimately the riders experienced the elevating passage by aqueduct over the Shawsheen River. This brought them to Billerica Pond, the dammed part of the summit-crest Concord River. Then, after crossing the pond and descending through locks to the Merrimack River, they could go about their business in newly industrialized Lowell. They might also spend the night at the widely known Middlesex Tavern before catching the morning boat back to Boston. All for the boat fare of 75 cents.

The question of economic success, when put before merchants and business agents, also elicited a positive response. Take a merchant who chose the canal to ship, say, 80 tons of material from Boston up to Middlesex Village for sale and get back 40 tons of produce, also by canal, for sale at harborside. He would save $292.10 over a traditional-minded rival who might have carried out the same scheme by land. This savings takes into account both what the land-traveling merchant would have paid for his teamsters ($480) and what the canal-inclined agent would have paid for horse and canalboat plus skipper and crew ($187.90). And this savings (discovered by Mary Stetson Clarke in the course of her researchings in the canal company's records) stands forth as the key to the canal's popularity among business interests. The canal gave businessmen a potent advantage, grand enough to advance the society from one social level to another.

And so the busy canalboats—most pulled by horse and mule, for this was a "traction" canal as opposed to those waterways on which sail- or pole-powered craft were found—contributed to the enrichment of merchants and landowners. Yet the problem remained of those increasingly expensive repairs, not to mention the competition. For where in post-Revolutionary America did one profitable system appear without stimulating a rival?

As the first decades of the nineteenth century rolled on, that competition came slowly, surely, overwhelmingly from one source—the newly introduced Boston & Lowell Railroad. As early as 1829 this entity appeared to the canal's proprietors as a "Giant," fully prepared to "swallow the canals." Ironically, the most advantageous route for the railroad was suggested to its backers by James F. Baldwin, one of Loammi's energetic and talented sons. He had been asked to prepare a survey and, going back to his father's desk, found the still-valid land surveys prepared under Loammi's directions. These he gave to the railroad-builders . . . the canal leading the way. Yet, in fact, the two modes of transportation worked along together for many years, the Middlesex not expiring until 1853.

Loammi himself, the Revolutionary colonel and great builder of the Middlesex, died but five years after the completion of his canal, exhausted by his labors. James Sullivan also died in that same year, 1808, undoubtedly with the conviction that, enriched by the canal, his heirs and those of his fellow stockholders would go on to dominate the prosperous region for generations.

In terms of return to stockholders, the canal also did fairly well, though the outlook seemed doubtful for years. It happened that the deaths of Baldwin and Sullivan in the same year and the occurrence soon thereafter of the depressive Jefferson embargo, followed by the disruptive War of 1812, served to drive the canal stock's value down, down from the height of $500 in 1804 to $300 in 1816. The flower appeared to have bloomed early, then faded. By the 1830s, however, dividends in the range of $25 to $30 a year were coming in and the curve was going back up; stockholders tended to conclude that their forebears' initial investment had been shrewd, and of course patriotic.

In the very long run, it must be admitted that the investment proved no great bonanza. As Mary Stetson Clarke adds up the figures, total dividends and eventual settlements with stockholders came to $559.50 a share—$180.50 less than the initial cost plus subsequent assessments. That, of course, says nothing about how the stockholder may have been able to leverage other opportunities as a result of his privileged ownership of these pieces of paper.

Also, in the reckoning of historian Henry Sinclair Drago, the cumulative bill to the stockholders of $750 was just about the same as the final payment to them made by the Boston & Lowell when that railroad acquired all shares in 1843. One suspects from all this that even the gloomiest of the original Boston financiers counted the gains (particularly the generational enhancement of land values and the boosting of various family businesses) as justifying the somewhat rash gamble.

There is certainly no historical doubt about the sudden booming of the Boston-Lowell industrial area. Obviously the Middlesex Canal was the trick, the economic spring that impelled this stupendous economic surge. In addition, something happened to the society of the region—a distinct break from the past. The old world of John Hancock and Loammi Baldwin, with Federalist estates maintained by servants and canalside agricultural laborers, seemed suddenly to be a thing of the past. Now there were new jobs, different clothes, other ways of behaving and being entertained. All these may be read as signs of a developing middle class, peasants no more.

Along the canal, the favorite spot for the newly leisured men and women of this altered society was buccolic Horn Pond. A pavilion of striped canvas and waving flags had been set up, as well as a bowling alley and a "bathing house." These stood near the canal's sequence of three locks; passengers could assemble here for that new event a "picnic." A band played, refreshments were served, and three nearby taverns offered a full range of gustatory delights. Adding to the colorful scene, Indians strolled among the crowd, offering baskets, sweetgrass brushes, and other crafts for sale. It was a world changing fast.

Some of the Yankees who have left diary accounts of these enjoyments may be recognized as members of the upper crust and intellectual elite—Edward Everett Hale, Eliza Quincy, and Henry David Thoreau. But other literary scraps have come down through time written by less notable, equally happy visitors to the pond. These people, to whom the word "humble" no longer applied, also took part in marching bands on excursions, in Sunday school parties, in outings with their children. And of course there were the businessmen and salesmen going to and fro. For them all, the canal was the way of moving, of being out with others, of sharing this new passage.

Author and clergyman Hale wrote many years later after this scene, too, had passed: "The present generation does not know it but travelling on a canal is one of the most charming ways of travelling. . . . to sit on the deck a boat and see the country slide by you . . . is one of the exquisite luxuries."

Yet the middle class, whatever its virtues, is not without its snobbery. Further, when there is a social disruption—with some quickly achieving a new affluence and others still left in the dust—the norms that used to hold that society together tend to become strained. Typically, this notice appeared one day in 1827 among the many regulations that were posted by the canal company:

No black passenger can be allowed to go in the boat, as much dissatisfaction was manifest in the last Year in Consequence thereof, unless the same be a servant to some person on board the boat.

The Middlesex Canal may have accelerated social change in the Boston-Lowell region, but not for all.

Canals for America?

For the nation as a whole, the lesson of the Middlesex Canal was clear to see: canals *could* be constructed here, despite America's relative lack of capital, her dearth of engineers, her confused landscape, and her high costs of labor. An impressive economic gain could be made by investing in such an improvement—a gain accompanied by social advances.

In 1816, immediately after the War of 1812, the commissioners of the newly chartered Erie Canal sent observers to report in detail on successes and failures along the Middlesex route. The not always secure locks the soon-rotting wooden aqueducts, the lingering question of expense vs. income . . . what did these all add up to? The Erie commissioners also sent their bright young engineer Canvass White to England to study developments along the industrial canals there. And they heeded what Fulton and others had had to say about ancient canals as well as the Canal du Midi. But most of all they concentrated on the example of the Middlesex; it was right there, next door, and it worked.

CLAIMING THE WESTWARD EMPIRE

THE ORIGINS of the Erie Canal—the New York State man-made wonder which persuaded ambitious Americans elsewhere that trans-Appalachian canals were possible—lie cozily wrapped in myth, legend, and even a few threads of history. As one historian has remarked, the very success of this eye-opening canal tended to distort its history: everyone wanted to be its father. In the light of the waterway's troubled, nearly impossible beginnings, that latter desire for fatherhood seems almost ludicrous. Indeed, the story can be seen as a folk drama or people's opera, with the ultimate appearance onstage of the true father of the canal, De Witt Clinton, as the *deus ex machina*.

One of the grand stories of the canal's origins dates back to the danger-filled middle years of the American Revolution, when the would-be nation was under a three-way attack by British forces. The battalions of playwright-general "Johnny" Burgoyne were driving down from Canada toward Albany, intent on merging there with two other British columns, one of which was to sweep in from the west along the Mohawk River, the other of which would sail up the Hudson from New York City. When united, the British command would crush all American forces in the North. The First Continental Congress, shocked

53

by this military threat and by fears about the fighting strength of the rapidly retreating American units, sent Congressman Gouverneur Morris north from Philadelphia to assess and possibly repair the situation.

The legend goes that one night, while dining with American officers in a farmhouse not far from the site of the battle that would terminate Burgoyne's thrust, Gouverneur Morris uplifted the flagging spirits of those field commanders by presenting a vision of the waterway that would one day course across New York State and bind the former colonies into an integrated, vibrant nation. A listener reported that Morris spoke of the day "when the waters of the great western seas would, by the aid of man, break through their barriers and mingle with those of the Hudson." On their bosom they would bear flotillas of vessels carrying goods and passengers to and from the western territories.

A letter written by Morris some time later gives an idea of the language he probably used as he elevated the morale of the officers. "As yet," he wrote, "we only crawl along the outer shell of our country. The interior excels the part we inhabit in soil, in climate, in everything. The proudest empire in Europe is but a bubble compared to what America *will* be, *must* be, in the course of two centuries, perhaps of one." It would be the canal that would make possible that future wealth and power.

The officers went on to win their battle at Saratoga, and Gouverneur Morris (who served as chairman of the canal commission in the difficult years of 1810 to 1813) went on through early American history as one of those stalwart Federalists implacably opposed to the War of 1812, and to anything particularly democratic. But because of that farmhouse speech and his later service in the canal cause, he is often pictured as father of the canal.

Another claimant to the fatherhood title is the Irish-born engineer Christopher Colles. This energetic and articulate artillery officer in the Continental Army produced in 1785 a book entitled *Proposals for the Settlement of the State of New York,* which did much to convince skeptics that a canal from the Hudson to the lakes was feasible. Actually, Colles labored in something of an engineering tradition: in 1724, long before the Revolution, the royal governor of the colony of New York received a recommendation for a similar waterway from his surveyor-general, Cadwallader Colden. Another recommendation surfaced in 1768. But it would take more than a comprehension of engineering principles to get any such program financed and fulfilled. It would take a political genius, one with a naturalist's understanding of the lay of the land and a keen sense of that land's human history.

Although Elkanah Watson had come to know the state thoroughly since his move to Albany from New England, and although he had been among the first to see the potentials of the salt business near Syracuse as a way of funding the canal, he could hardly be called a political genius. With increased fervor as the eighteenth century ended, he attempted to goad local business interests to the point of action—in deliberate competition with the rest of the country. When it came to canals, he argued that "it appears that every natural advantage is in favor of New York." And he went on to speak fondly but disparagingly of "Father Washington" and that old man's preoccupation with the Potomac route.

Some years later, when the Erie Canal was under construction, Elkanah Watson came out with a book that hailed himself as the chief advocate of the New York route. It was he who had

first conceived the idea of the practicability of counteracting, at least by fair competition, the favourite plan Washington was then pursuing, with zeal and ardour, to allure all the trade of the western regions, connected with the Ohio and the Great Lakes—even the fur trade from Detroit—to Alexandria.

One doubts if Watson's disparagement of the President did much for his own credibility or popularity. At any rate, it was not Watson who had the moral character to rally the people of New York state to the cause of actually building the canal. No, that would require a man, one man joined by others, whose roots went deeper into the soil of the region. Namely, De Witt Clinton.

Iroquois Empire, German Vineyards

The grand historian of American's westward movements, Francis Parkman, called the Iroquois the "Romans of the New World." This was because of their political acumen; he recognized that the Iroquois of central New York originally had the most advanced form of government of any nation on this continent. They ruled not by majority but by consensus; through their "long house" style of democracy, they were able to bind together a more solidly integrated, militarily fit confederation of peoples than existed elsewhere among native Americans. The Iroquois referred to their democratic empire as the Five Nations. It's strangely appropriate that not far not from their confederation's Onondaga headquarters, in Oneida country, now stands the city of Rome, and that it was in Rome that the first shovelful of dirt for the bed of the Erie canal was dug. Romans indeed—but would their empire endure?

The Iroquois, as well as possessing a superior kind of government to hold their nations together, stood at what would become and remain the center of eastern North America's power network. In that sense also Parkman might have viewed them as Romans, for their empire commanded the heart of a continent, not Europe but America. Their area of control extended from Maine and Canada south to the Carolinas; it ranged west to the Great Lakes after their raids (commenced in 1642) subjugated the Eries and the Hurons.

At this time in the seventeenth century, the Iroquois numbered about sixteen thousand people. Though surrounded by the far more numerous Algonquians, they were universally feared for their stinging, brilliantly directed attacks. It happened that during the early explorations of Samuel de Champlain, he had the misfortune to engage the Iroquois in combat, thereby earning for France the eternal enmity of these pivotally positioned fighters. Of the Iroquois warriors, eternal allies of the British, an astonished French priest wrote: "They attack like lions. . . . They take flight like birds."

All of New France's attempts to unite her Canadian and Louisianan halves into a continental whole ran directly up against the hard-core opposition of the Iroquois, whose palisaded villages and alert scouts blocked almost every route south from Quebec and Montreal. Nevertheless, the French sought both to establish a fortress in the area of Pittsburgh (where they defeated and captured George Washington) and to outflank the Iroquois to the east by means of a bastion at Ticonderoga on Lake George. Against that thrust, for much of the seventeenth and eighteenth centuries, the Iroquois maintained a generally effective alliance with the English. Unfortunately for the later residents of the Mohawk Valley, this firm alliance extended through the time when the British became enemies of the Americans.

Yet before taking up arms in the Revolution, the settlers of the Mohawk Valley had to defend themselves against the ravages of the French and Indians Wars. The final phase of those wars began in 1755 when the British commander in chief in North America, Major General Edward Braddock, was overwhelmingly defeated in his attempt to remove the French from Pittsburgh's Fort Duquesne. Then, in one of their most damaging campaigns, the French under the Marquis de Montcalm struck on two fronts, first from the northwest down the Mohawk Valley, then from the northeast down Lake Champlain and Lake George. With these successes of 1756 and 1757, it appeared that the French and their Algonquian allies would win the continent. But in the following year a massive force of colonists and Highlanders and Iroquois under General John Forbes finally succeeded in taking Fort Duquesne. Only then could the British embark on the road to victory at Quebec; only then could their allies the Iroquois hope once more that their empire was secure.

A settlement in the Mohawk Valley with the peculiar name German Flats had borne the brunt of that campaign when French forces slammed into the heart of British territory from the west. The war on this front had begun in early 1756 when Montcalm brought his forces across Lake Ontario from Fort Frontenac and, marching up the Oswego River, overran British forces at Fort Bull. The fort stood almost exactly at the site where later, in the era of the Erie Canal, the village of Rome would be built; there Fish Creek, draining into Oneida Lake, affords access via a brief portage to the head of the Mohawk River. Having won this foothold position, the French had stormed on down the valley the next year, ravaging German Flats and making any would-be settlers from the east think twice about moving to the fringes of the Iroquois empire.

It had always been a valley of bloody contests. Albany, near the mouth of the Mohawk River, had had to fight for its life ever since the Dutch founded Fort Orange in 1623 and the English took it over in 1664. In the unforgotten French-inspired Indian attacks of 1698, both Albany and Schenectady (established farther upriver) had been designated "military towns"—that is, towns under military command in which all inhabitants had to recognize themselves as soldiers who might be executed if they abandoned their assigned posts. As the French and Indian Wars commenced and intensified in the next century, the little farming communities up the valley came to know what the ringing of the church bell meant:

another attack on people and property. The citizens of German Flats lived within that fearful tradition.

But who were these Germans of the Flats, these settlers who returned again and again to their blackened, smoking villages to start rebuilding them? Who were these people called Germans who epitomized all early Americans fighting for their land? They were not the freeboooting fur traders nor the raffish squawmen of the frontier; they were farmers, blacksmiths, tanners, citizens male and female. From their perspective, the continent on which they moved belonged neither to the great European powers nor to the Indians. It belonged to them; they would certainly fight for it.

"Bush Germans" they were called by some of their more refined English-speaking neighbors. "Industrious Teutons" they were called by a historian who took particular interest in the business established by one of their communities in the vicinity of German Flats, at Little Falls. Here enterprising men and boys had found a way to haul the riverboats up around the falls through the surrrounding swamps. It was no canal, but it was a beginning. From that industrious community would come Nicholas Herkimer, hero of Oriskany, the Revolutionary battle fought before Saratoga to prevent the western British column from meeting with General Burgoyne.

The ancestors of Herkimer and his neighbors had stemmed from the part of Germany known as the Rhenish Palatinate, a bountiful territory along the Rhine which French forces had devastated on Louis XIV's direct orders in 1688. Hundreds of farmer families, their vineyards destroyed, had no choice but to emigrate to the New World. Arriving in New York, many of them found not employment but indentured servitude among the wealthy Dutch and English families along the Hudson. There the "Palatines" were engaged in the demanding task of producing tar and other naval stores from forests bordering the river and within the Catskills. When that industry failed, some of the men were impressed as seamen and soldiers, and many family members died of starvation. A number of survivors found their ways to the Mohawk and Schoharie valleys. Hacking out homesteads for themselves from this near-wilderness, they thereby put their claim on the land through which the Erie Canal would run a century and more later.

By the late eighteenth century, after recovery from the brutalities of the French and Indian Wars and in the decades before the onset of the Revolution, the raw little German settlements had become bustling farm communities. The business of hauling boats around the falls—carrying them either on sleds that could be slid through the swamps or on wheeled carts for land passage—allowed certain families, among them the Herkimers, to flourish. The valley farmers won a much-deserved reputation for the quality of their wine and produce (particularly the cheese), though the deliberate pace of their special way of life seemed quaintly old-fashioned to visiting Yankees.

Traces of the distinctive architecture and cultural patterns of these people can be found by travelers along the canal today in the town of Herkimer, in Palatine Bridge, and in several communities on either side of Little Falls. In that small yet distinguished city, one spies a sign for the "Bierstube" and can visit the Herkimer home. Unfortunately the wonderful octagonal church that once stood here, looking as if it had been heli-lifted directly over from the old country, was recently taken down. Even more unfortunately, the German spirit, like that of the Iroquois, exists here only in the form of memories.

Bugles at Fort Stanwix

At the head of the valley, near Fort Bull and the eventual site of Rome, stood Fort Stanwix, defender in pre-Revolutionary times of a region that had already had more than its share of battles. The down-valley German farmers, colonial Americans of a distinctive stripe, viewed the British military goings-on at the fort with mistrust and disapproval: these over-lords obviously gave a higher priority to imperial strategies (which were focused on the securing of the western fur trade among the Iroquois) than to defending them or developing the territory. They saw the epitome of that attitude in Sir William Johnson, who, though a knighted hero of the French and Indian Wars, seemed to the Palatines little more than a clever Irish settler who had won his way to wealth and power by taking as one of his wives the sister of a reigning Mohawk sachem. "Johnson of the Mohawks," indeed. Sir William's pro-native attitude galled his farmer neighbors, whether of German or English descent. They wished to hunt,

59

to push the red men aside, to settle farther and farther west, to exercise all possible freedom upon the land they considered theirs. Of this freewheeling spirit, Johnson wrote: "I have daily to contend with thousands who, by their avarice, cruelty, or indiscretion, are constantly contradicting all judicious measures with the Indians."

However unpopular his policies, Sir William had become a figure of immense authority. Officially, he was general superintendent of all Indian affairs north of the Ohio River—which is another way of saying that he was Britain's ambassador plenipotentiary to the Iroquois. Personally, he was lord of the baronial Johnson Hall (located at Johnstown, 15 miles downriver from Palatine Bridge), where he played host to the numbers of Mohawks and western Iroquois who continued to drift up and down the valley. The Mohawks, perhaps it needs to be said, spoke an Algonquian language but constituted one of the Iroquois' Five Nations; they were "guardians of the [empire's] eastern door."

In 1768, Sir William Johnson convened at Fort Stanwix a grand meeting of officials and native American leaders for the signing of a treaty that represented basic British policy in the wake of the French and Indian War. From all the Five Nations and other, neighboring peoples came an estimated 3,400 delegates. Recognizing this treaty-signing as the most solemn of occasions, the assembled decked themselves out in spectacular finery. Some two hundred canoes were needed to transport the gifts alone. With a discharge of firearms and a blaring of bugles, the meeting began.

The purpose of the treaty, Sir William announced, was to modify the Proclamation Line of 1763, which had been drawn from Canada to Georgia down the ridge of the Appalachians. The line went directly through Fort Stanwix, separating Great Britain's American colonies to the east from the Iroquois and other nations to the west. By the terms of that proclamation, the Indians had been stripped of all land that lay to the east, and the colonists had been banned from establishing any settlements to the west of the line. Now, Johnson announced, the line was going to be bent more to the west; it would run down the Unadilla River to the Susquehanna, thence to Pittsburgh and along the Ohio to the Mississippi. In addition, large parts of the "Indian Reserve" were to be opened up for white settlement. Having wined and dined his native allies lavishly, Johnson gave them no option but to sign the treaty.

It was a masterful performance, conducted with great skill by an officer who knew just how far he could go. Both Johnson himself and the British crown were determined not to alienate the Iroquois and to keep the western territories in their hands, because the Iroquois were the key element in the central business of catching and processing the beaver and other fur-bearing animals. But the British, in stressing that essentially pro-Iroquois policy, ran counter to the inclinations of most colonists. These eighteenth-century Americans, including the Palatines, saw the West not as an Indian reserve but as the land of their present expectations and future settlement. They were not interested in the kind of peace that the crown wanted to impose, whereby all trading and all other dealings with the Indians would be managed by such royal agents as Sir William. They were certainly not interested in further enriching Johnson and his heirs and cronies.

When Sir William died in 1774, the crown went one step further in alienating the settlers of New York and other west-facing colonies. It passed the notorious Quebec Act, which transferred all authority for dealing with the Iroquois into the hands of royal officials based in Quebec. This act is paired by many historians with Britain's imposition of the tea tax on the Thirteen Colonies as a prime cause of the American Revolution. The behavior of the colonists certainly justifies this view. In Boston, patriotic citizens staged their Tea Party; on the New York frontier, settlers took their rifles down from the wall and joined patriotic militia bands.

Not all settlers, to be sure, favored the cause of independence. Many men of the frontier chose to follow Johnson's son and son-in-law, Sir John Johnson and Guy Johnson, in their loyalty to the old colonial patterns. When dislodged from the valley and from Fort Stanwix by the patriots, these American loyalists became Tory raiders, slipping skillfully, ferociously down the riverways of New York from bases in Canada, always accompanied by Iroquois partners. The early years of the Revolution were years of flaming terror for the Palatines and other Mohawk Valley settlers.

Here the Revolution—the war that would determine the ownership of the land on which the canal would be built—took on a rather strange cast. This was not a revolution of radicals against monarchists, of lowest-class members fighting heroically against dragoons hired by the highest class. No, it was a war of neighbor against neighbor (as so unforgettably portrayed in Walter Edmonds's *Drums Along the Mohawk*), of farmers against traders, of isolated white settlers against highly mobile red woodsmen. But, however the war was viewed, its real losers would be those wondrous "Romans," the Iroquois who had possessed an empire.

Mixed News from Oriskany

Though a small piece of the total American Revolution, this particular piece helped determine victory. New York State, for all its later leadership and grandeur, was then a rather questionable contributor to the cause of nationhood. In New York City, certain radicals had initially challenged the magnificent aristocrats who controlled the mercantile life of the harbor. But when General William Howe and Admiral Richard Howe swung into the city in 1776 after the British evacuation from Boston, New York became quite contentedly neutralized. The contention of certain up-country patriots against the regime of Guy Johnson—even their seizing and rebuilding of Fort Stanwix—seemed a parochial and negligible matter.

It must be added that the patroons and other estate holders immediately upriver from New York City became revolutionaries also—revolutionaries of sorts. As well as being intellectually inclined toward freedom, they figured (as did their counterparts in Virginia) that liberation from Britain could win them even more power. Yet the support they gave the Revolution was hardly in keeping with their might; they did little to protect fellow New Yorkers from the torchings and destructions that were reported up and down the Mohawk and Schoharie valleys.

As the situation on that front worsened, the Palatines and other harassed settlers begged for assistance from the Continental Congress, from Colonel John Stark's New Hampshire militiamen, from any source. Eventually a small force under Peter Gansevoort and Marinus Willet was dispatched to take charge of Fort Stanwix. But still the terrifying raids continued, with increasing brutality. Nothing could be done, it seemed, to stop them.

Then early in the summer of 1777 came the news of Britain's three-pronged attack upon the northern colonies from north, west, and south. This was the moment when Gouverneur Morris was sent from Philadelphia by Congress to bolster the morale of troops retreating before the south-thrusting point of General Burgoyne's sword. It was also at this tense moment that Nicholas Herkimer mounted his farm horse and rallied fellow settlers to march up the Mohawk Valley to the support of the tiny American force at "Fort Schuyler," as it had been hopefully renamed.

As July ended and August began, the fort had suffered the full brunt of the eastward-sweeping British attack force. The British columns were led by Barry St. Leger, a brilliant brigadier general who had shone at Quebec in the last war. Now he commanded an army combined of battle-trained regulars, Tories bent on revenge, and Iroquois bound to reclaim their valley—seventeen hundred men in all. It seemed thoroughly unlikely that Gansevoort and Willet could hold out against him.

To their aid hurried General Herkimer's five hundred citizen soldiers, accompanied by a handful of friendly Oneidas. This native nation, on whose land Fort Schuyler was located, had reviewed the option offered at the beginning of the war by Iroquois leadership: each of the Five Nations could join either side. The Oneidas chose to forsake the Johnson clique, to split the Five Nations apart, and to trust those white Americans who were talking freedom. In this courageous decision they were joined by the Tuscaroras, who had recently been subjected to British maltreatment, then adopted by the sympathetic Oneidas. The impact of this splitting apart of the Iroquois was profound. In the words of contemporary observers, it was then that "the light in the longhouse went out."

Before taking command of his little band of allies, Nicholas Herkimer had earned the respect of most patriotic settlers, both in the course of his successful life as citizen and businessman and in the weekly drills which he and his officers imposed on the youths of the valley. But some still viewed him, with his German mode of speech and his methodical approach to this desperate march, as ludicrously antique. They all knew that the British siege of Fort Schuyler, which had begun on August 3, was a critical matter: if the fort fell, the entire valley would surely follow and St. Leger's linkup with Burgoyne would be unstoppable. This led some of the hotter-blooded settlers to want to break ranks and charge ahead. Why try to figure out the enemy's counterplan? Why was the general pausing and listening to rumors from his scouts? Save the fort!

The scouts' rumors focused on a large, Tory-led Iroquois force that was possibly setting a trap for the onrushing Americans. But despite

Herkimer's orders to proceed cautiously and prepare for a battle at a favorable site, a number of headstrong Americans continued to crash ahead, up the trail and down into the tight valley of Oriskany Creek. There, near present-day Utica, the trap had been set; now it was sprung. Perhaps if Herkimer's orders had been followed, the valleymen could have acquitted themselves better. But as it was, they had to fight from tree to tree, outnumbered and disordered, falling by the score before the guns of the Tories and their allies.

Herkimer himself was wounded in the leg. He was bleeding copiously and was unable to stand, but, demonstrating courage and command, he kneeled on a stump (in a pose that a sculptor has made famous) and lit a pipe as he allowed his leg to be bandaged. He continued to issue a stream of orders, directing his depleted force to fight together and make every shot count. And so they survived, survived to retreat. Yet at Oriskany the American colonists gave as much punishment as they received, with the result that the Tory-led force returned to the siege with no sense of triumph. These rebels could fight.

Furthermore, the Continental Congress had finally recognized the importance of the Mohawk Valley. To the New Yorkers' aid and for the relief of the siege at Fort Schuyler, they finally sent a small army of Continentals under the command of Benedict Arnold. Though Arnold was still smarting from having been passed over for the rank of major general (a rank which he finally did receive, before Oriskany), he was undoubtedly the most attack-minded of George Washington's generals. The word that he was preparing to proceed up the Mohawk was exactly the news that the bloodied valleymen had been waiting for.

Arnold's reputation was mighty enough to make the invaders think twice about continuing their siege of the strategic fort. But neither that reputation by itself nor the brave performance of Herkimer's men at Oriskany would seem potent enough to bring about the British retreat that then—rather mysteriously—occurred. There was another benign force at work. The Iroquois massed at Fort Schuyler somehow came to believe that a huge army of patriot-allied native Americans was being led by Arnold. Who were these spectral warriors? Algonquians? Tuscaroras? Historians have no idea.

Spooked by this imagined army, bands of Iroquois began to melt away from St. Leger and the Tories. On August 22, the siege was lifted; St. Leger retired back down the Oswego to Lake Ontario. Benedict Arnold, given a victory he had not earned, could go on to win a real one (with some help from Colonel Stark and General Gates) at Saratoga. This was, unarguably, the key battle of the Revolution, the one that encouraged the French to come in on our side. Ahead lay Yorktown.

The End of the Iroquois

Still the raids continued, increasingly vicious; scalping and torture became the order of the day. In both New York State and Pennsylvania, Indians and Loyalists used local knowledge to make canny strikes at out-lying farms and settlements, growing ever bolder. The year of 1788 was special misery for the people of the valley: German Flats was utterly de-stroyed, and in nearby Cherry Valley (to reach it from Palatine Bridge, one went up Canajoharie Creek and over the ridge) thirty unarmed villagers were massacred.

The American military command, outraged by these assaults and emboldened by victories in the northern states, determined to secure the frontier. A massive campaign was planned, whereby two forces of about fifteen hundred Continentals each would sweep into Iroquois country. The first, under New York's James Clinton (father of De Witt) was to follow the route from the Mohawk Valley over the ridge to Cherry Valley; the second, under John Sullivan (brother of the Merrimack Canal's James Sullivan), would strike north from Pennsylvania up the Susquehanna River. At the border of New York and Pennsylvania the two forces would merge for a final assault up along Seneca Lake and west to Genesee Castle. (The names of many Iroquois villages were coupled with the word "Castle," signifying a militarily defended position.) In the parlance of military strategists, the Continentals' two-pronged assault was to be a campaign "by fire and sword," deliberately destructive and vengeful.

Neither the war-torn region in which the campaign occurred nor the families of the men who participated in it ever quite recovered from its horrors. Memory of its blood and slaughter would live on in this part of New York State, somewhat like the memory of battle in the South after the Civil War. The beating of "drums along the Mohawk" would always

65

be heard. So would the remembered adventures live on, the mythic feats, helping to form the characters of the next, canal-building generation and of the people as a distinctive culture. In the case of De Witt Clinton, it seems altogether likely that one episode in the dramatic story of his father's campaign among the Iroquois made an impression on him.

Having led his columns of marching men over the ridge to the massacre site at Cherry Valley, General Clinton faced the problem of continuing on through the tangled hills and valleys of southern New York State in time to meet with the force of his superior, General Sullivan, as planned. This summer of 1779 happened to be a particularly dry one. And because General Clinton's best bet for speedy passage to the south was to take advantage of the region's rivers and lakes by means of the portable boats he had brought along, the drought threatened his advance. At one point when his amphibious force was sailing down Otsego Lake (at the end of which Cooperstown is located today), word came to Clinton that the lake's outflow, the critical link to the Susquehanna River, was too shallow to permit the passage of the boats. Demonstrating a familiarity with hydraulics that would do his own son proud, the general proposed a radical solution: the river would be dammed; then, after the level of the lake at the southern end had risen 3 feet, the dam would be destroyed, and the boats would ride the crest of the released wave down to the Susquehanna.

It was an ingenious, if rustic, solution; General Clinton, after what must have been a thrilling ride, made it to the rendezvous on time. But it was by no means a pleasurable campaign. The British-allied Iroquois fought fiercely, then were totally routed by the well-organized Americans.

After the two armies of Clinton and Sullivan had united and had won victories at Chemung and Newtown at the end of August, the way was opened for assault on a grand scale. Under attack, the Senecas (westernmost of the Five Nations) fled from their towns; the native villages and castles were burned and leveled, one after another, whatever military sense that made. Within a few weeks the American soldiers succeeded in destroying 160,000 bushels of corn, and uncountable acres of apple-ripe orchards, even though the neighboring settlers were starving and eating roots. Civilians and braves alike fell before the onrushing army.

Those Iroquois who survived the blitzkrieg now saw in their future only death by starvation or complete dependency upon the newly dominant Americans. Many of them fled to Canada; many starved on the way north. The empire that had controlled the continent would no longer be theirs—it would belong to the people with the more powerful weapons. Along with the weapons and tools of that technologically superior society went the money sense and the aggressive inclination to make grand, unnatural things happen.

The Yankee Dimension

The German-descended valleymen industriously went about reclaiming their ravaged farms, rebuilding their blackened villages. As their woods rang again to the sound of axes, as their fields woke again to the caress of wooden plows, these villagers and farmers must have taken joy in the land they had helped win from the British and the Iroquois. They had no way of knowing how soon they too would lose it.

The personality of the Mohawk Valley, its ethnic and social character, began to change immediately after the Revolution. Spilling across the Hudson River and spreading up the valley like an infestation of killer bees came Yankees by the hundreds and thousands. Leaving their hillside farms behind them in Connecticut, Massachusetts, and Vermont, these Yankee migrants sought the deeper soils and larger prospects of New York. Ultimately more than a million of them swarmed in—the first of America's great migrations.

And if anyone chooses to believe that the physical quality of the land itself determines the social development of a nation rather than the other way around, here's a glittering example on that side the argument. For it was the spotty soil of New England that determined who went over the Hudson and became "Yankee-Yorkers" and built the Yankee-looking towns. These were by no means the contented and conservative New Englanders of the seacoast and of the wealth-producing valleys. They were, by contrast, unsuccessful hill farmers, and a discontented and quirky lot they were.

In the early days of colonial settlement these primitive agriculturalists had chosen hillside sites in central and western New England. At first their choice seemed sensible: here trees were easier to clear; wide-sweeping vistas provided defense against Indian attacks. But within a few decades those accessible acres proved good for nothing but sheep.and goats. Ever discontent, ever trusting in greener pastures beyond the horizon, the failed farmers took off westward, taking with them their cleverness and their multitudes of children. The sprawling Vermont family of Joseph Smith (founder of the Church of Latter-Day Saints) may be seen as rather typical of those who undertook the journey—the father a tinkerer, the mother industrious and socially ambitious.

On the far side of the Hudson and up the Mohawk Valley the immigrating families found both magnificent soil for their farms and a new liberty for their spirits. Here, freed from the old Puritan strictures, they let both their religious imaginations and their land-grabbing tendencies fly free. To these speculators and immigrants, the German villagers, always short of cash, sold out in town after town. Some of the Palatine families moved west, ahead of the wave, beyond abandoned Fort Schuyler. Only out there, in the words of a character in *Drums Along the Mohawk,* could a German villager find "no pushing Yankees to remind you that the organized [i.e., Federal] army and the New England states had seized the reins of government" during the war. After that, those victorious Yankees took over the political and cultural destiny of the state.

Perhaps it was unfair to liken these invaders to killer bees. But take the little valley town of Mohawk, a few miles upstream from Little Falls and across the river from Herkimer. The town had been decimated in the raids of the French and Indian Wars, ravaged by Tories and Iroquois during the Revolution, rebuilt and rebuilt unflaggingly by the Palatines. By the 1790s it and many other towns like it along the lower river had been totally taken over by Yankee occupiers. Thus when the Erie Canal was built, there were few German families, few descendants of the old, embattled heroes, to benefit from the valley's new affluence.

By 1800—seventeen years before the first shovelful was dug for the Erie Canal—there were almost as many Yankees living in New York State as in Connecticut. These were the aggressive, inventive people who, in dramatic contrast to the leisurely Palatines, would sweep New York State into the new century with the energy of a housewife in spring. Yet it would certainly be a mistake to mock the qualities which the Yankees brought to New York State along with their religious eccentricities and their platoons of children. In the words of one admiring historian, "the new aristocracy of wealth" which developed in this central region of the state consisted "mostly of New Englanders."

On his tour of New York State, Timothy Dwight called the region a colony of New England. Then he went on to say appreciatively that New York now had all the "sprightliness, thrift, and beauty of New England." The conquest was quite complete.

Heyday of the Speculators

Those who now expectantly moved up the Mohawk Valley did so at a joltingly slow pace. Even on the smoothest stretch—where a concatenation of local landowners might have prompted the building of a toll road—teamsters could cover no more than 20 miles in one wrenching day. The road-builders did everything they could to facilitate western movement, as did the tavern-builders, but the journey remained a challenge for oxen and humans alike. Nonetheless, in and across New York streamed the would-be farmers, the would-be sellers of everything, and most notably the would-be land speculators large and small.

From Rome, whose recently laid-out streets throbbed with business and construction near ruined Fort Schuyler, an Indian trail ran west, showing the way. Improved but slightly and called the Genesee Road, it carried travelers to the destroyed Iroquois village on the Genesee River; beyond that, following a ridge that marked the separation point of limestone and granite geologies, the trail proceeded up and over the Niagara escarpment to a junction near the site of present-day Buffalo, then on to Fort Niagara. In these western territories beyond the Finger Lakes, travelers were actually in land that had been claimed by Massachusetts since earliest colonial times. But finally, in 1786, a compromise was worked out whereby Massachusetts yielded its political claims in order to capitalize on the vast tracts—a source of revenue desperately needed by the war-battered eastern state.

So it happened that two Boston speculators named Oliver Phelps and Nathaniel Gorham became the possessors of all land to the west of the "Pre-emption Line," which ran south from Lake Ontario to the Pennsylvania border at about the east-west position of present-day Geneva. For these 6 million acres, they were to pay about 3 cents an acre. But, like

69

many other would-be speculators, Messrs. Phelps and Gorham did not quite have the money when it came time to pay up. The vast barony thus passed into the hands of Philadelphia banker Robert Morris, a signer of the Declaration of Independence and the alleged "financier of the Revolution." Yet even for this high-class speculator, it was too big a deal. Failing to meet the terms of payment, Morris was hustled off to debtors' prison, where he remained from 1798 until 1801; nor was he ever to regain his former fortunes.

A Baltimore speculator with the significant name of Nathaniel Rochester then had better luck. On the acreage that he acquired within the original Phelps-Gorham territory, above the falls of the Genesee River, would be built the town that became the most booming city along the Erie Canal—Rochester. Into much of the rest of that territory moved English and Dutch investors, for Europe still remained the home of most of the world's big money.

Between that westernmost region of New York State and the already claimed areas east of Rome, many smaller speculators and developers tried to make their real estate dreams come true. The government of the state, overburdened with war debts, was eager to sell off to these busy buyers every last acre. Even the few remaining Iroquois found themselves caught up in the land-sales excitement. They seized on the opportunity to get something tangible for hereditary territories which the new Americans would, predictably, snatch away from them sooner or later. Then they headed sadly north, joining the others who had already established Iroquois centers in Canada.

To Market, to Market

The ultimate small purchaser of acres within this Erie Canal region was, of course, the homesteading farmer. Having signed a paper of seemingly impossible terms under the old landholder's eyes, he strode or rode to the appointed portion of wilderness, his now the life of killing trees and selling crops to meet payments. And what remarkable landsmen these homesteaders were. The most vigorous of them cleared and planted 10 acres in the first year of their occupancy. That maximum accomplishment did not leave time, however, for the settler to build a house for his down-valley bride. Most of the couples, working on their log-and-board cabins at the same time, could clear and plant but 4 acres a year. Clearings merged, becoming farm country; wilderness turned into townships. Some of the more rugged frontiersmen (particularly the hunters and trappers), appalled at the wilderness-turned-village, took off for the West.

There is the hallowed myth about the self-sufficient all-American farmer: with goods produced on his land, he happily weathers all storms and remains removed from the world's economic-political hassles. Not in New York State. Here the objective of the late-eighteenth- and early-nineteenth-century farmer, as pointed out by New York historian David Ellis, was not to achieve self-sufficiency but to escape it. He could pay for his land and translate his prodigious work into an adequate living only by integrating himself with the nation's economy. And that could only be done by *shipping* his produce—meaning, in western New York State, mostly wheat (or possibly syrup or potash)—to the distant down-valley market.

The Yankee-Yorker farmers looked to the brutal toll road as the essential link between them and the market. Down this boggy, rocky, rutted road to the city jolted their sacks and kegs of produce. The primitive, delapidated wooden wagons were driven by teamsters who made perhaps $30 a year, until their bodies too were broken. It was the way life had always been: the farmers worked with ages-old equipment, used soil-punishing agricultural techniques, relied on the whims of a distant economic system to return to them the wherewithal for tools and seed. Always they were at the mercy of the damagingly high transportation rates.

No wonder that Elkanah Watson, when he made his tour of the state in 1788, spotted improved transportation as they key to economic progress. Among the influential gentlemen to whom the Albany businessman communicated this strong conviction were Senator (former General) Philip Schuyler and Governor George Clinton (brother of De Witt's dam-building father James). They heard with sympathy Watson's argument that the most direct way to accomplish internal improvement was to assist the passage of boats up and down the Mohawk River. Schuyler and Clinton had the power to make things happen in the state legislature . . . whether or not they bought Watson's entire concept of a state-spanning canal.

Cleverly crafted by Senator Schuyler and Governor Clinton, a Mohawk Improvement Bill passed through the state legislature in 1791 despite heavy opposition from downstate delegates. The secret to the bill's success was that the Mohawk proposal was tied to the creation of yet another, more popular canal in the north. The intent of the total package was to unite the state (meaning its products and its markets) by joined waterways. Just as one transportation company was to fund and build a system that would link the Hudson with Seneca Lake via the Mohawk, so the other company would link the Hudson with Lake Champlain. Down the route from the west would come agricultural produce; from the north, iron.

With purposes similar to those of the Boston aristocrats who had undertaken the Middlesex Canal for the enrichment of their region and themselves, Philip Schuyler and his partners (who called themselves the Western Inland Lock Navigation Company) set about planning their westward-reaching waterway. But whereas the builders of the Middlesex had dug an independent channel, having carefully surveyed the region to find the easiest grandients, here the builders employed by Schuyler chose to work with all the known hazards and shifting uncertainties of the Mohawk River channel. These included the 200-foot declivity at Cohoes Falls near the mouth of the Mohawk and the blockage at Little Falls, 75 miles upriver.

At Little Falls, Senator Schuyler and his wealthy friends proceeded to construct a mile-long canal with five locks of 9 lift-feet each, adequate to raise boats up, over, and around the rocky rapids. The directors of the Western Inland seemed to have every confidence that with land sales booming in the west and with the increase of agriculture, the payback from freight traffic would turn their costly engineering project into a financially sound investment. They ignored repeated observations from Elkanah Watson and others that European experience showed it would be preferable to construct a wholly independent channel (and to aim not at a limited objective like Seneca Lake, or even Lake Ontario, but to go all the way to Lake Erie, to connect the seas). No, this was still the era of shorter-term solutions. That appeared to be the only way to take America West, by little, practical steps.

After a false start or two, the directors followed the by then standard maneuver of retaining William Weston to be their engineer. He immedi-

The floating bridge on Massachusetts's Middlesex Canal, *above,* allowed tow horses to cross the mill pond at Billerica. *Detail of painting from Billerica Historical Society*

Below left, the 1795 "Hampshire Machine" lifted carts carrying canal barges up an inclined plane, above falls on the Connecticut River. *American Canal and Transportation Center*

Below right, the diagrams show how classic European locks with V-gates at either end assisted a boat passing upriver. *American Canal and Transportation Center*

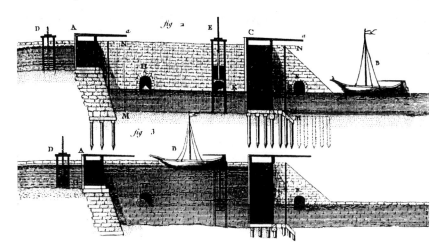

On the facing page: Above, paralleling the river, the Erie Canal runs east-west along the Mohawk Valley. *Below,* at Profile Rock near Little Falls, the canal and river squeeze through the valley's narrowest point. *Erie Canal Museum photos*

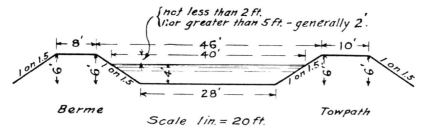

1817
Section of Original Erie as built.
Note 8 ft. berme instead of 5 ft. as specified.

Berme

Towpath

Scale 1 in. = 20 ft.

The cut-away drawing, *above,* shows the engineering plan for the original Erie Canal, built 1817–25. *Below,* a survey map of 1747 shows the location of the Five Iroquois Nations—directly along the route of the later canal.

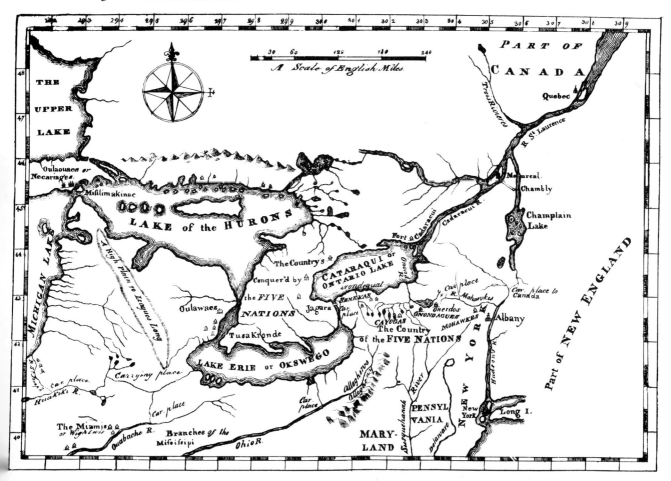

On the facing page: Above, a nineteenth-century engraving by John Hill depicts the crucial junction of the west-reaching Erie Canal (foreground) and north-stretching canal to Lake Champlain. *Below,* Hill's contemporary, William Rackerby Miller, painted the sentimental view of Little Falls on the canal. *New York Historical Society* and *Albany Institute of History and Art*

John Wesley Jarvis portrayed the Erie's De Witt Clinton at age 55, one year before the canal's completion, four years before the governor's death. *New York Historical Society*

On the facing page: Workmen in bowlers lounge on balance beams that open the gates of the engineering masterpiece of the Erie, the locks at Lockport. *Lockport Historical Society*

The plan and section for the construction at Lockport show the arrangement of the five double locks. *Lockport Historical Society*

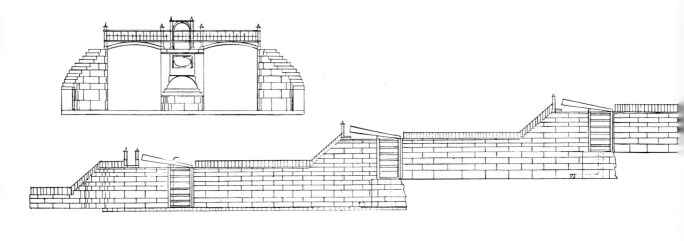

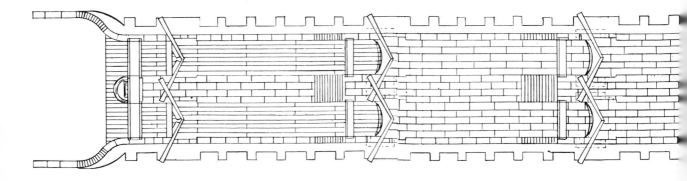

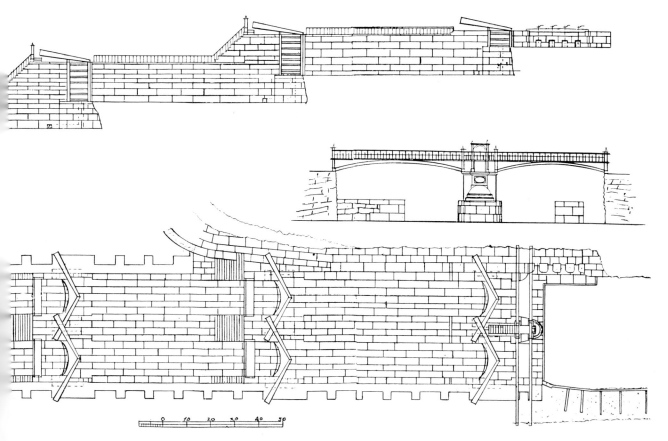

On the facing page: Above, one proud canal family poses with its broad-beamed line barge—the owner/skipper, mother/cook, boy/hoggee. *Below,* a group of canalside workmen display the tools of their trades for camera and posterity. *Erie Canal Museum photos*

In a lamp-lit cabin, brother and sister, who attended school only when the canal was closed in winter, are drilled on their books by mother. *Erie Canal Museum*

The mules, *above and below,* are being prodded aboard the barge over a special gangplank, then urged by tail-lift down to the stable in the bow of the boat. *Erie Canal Museum photos*

East-bound "Buffalo," pictured above, passes a west-bound barge above the lock. Occasionally, low water would cause jams and groundings ("mudlarkings"). *Erie Canal Museum photos*

Above, among the last structures completed on the Erie, "weighlocks," like this one at Rochester, weighed the barge's load by water displacement. *Below,* costly Black River Canal was one of the first links commissioned after the Erie opened in 1825. *Erie Canal Museum photos*

Maryland's Chesapeake and Ohio Canal paralleled the Potomac, locking boats up through both rocky passes, *above,* and peaceful glens, *below. C&O Canal National Monument photos*

Eleven stone aqueducts, like the one above, had to be built to carry the Chesapeake and Ohio Canal cross-country from Georgetown to Cumberland, where barges took on coal for the trip home, *below*. *C&O Canal National Monument photos*

On the facing page: Above, Virginia's James & Kanawha Canal brought up-country goods down to Richmond. The chart, *below,* shows lifts and levels of the Portage Railroad, which lifted and lowered Pennsylvania's canal systems over the Alleghenies. *New York Public Library* and *Allegheny Portage Railroad National Historic Site*

PROFILE of OLD ALLEGHENY PORTAGE RAILROAD

BEGUN	MAR. 26, 1831
IN SERVICE	MAR. 18, 1834
ABANDONED	JULY 1, 1855
DISMANTLED	1858

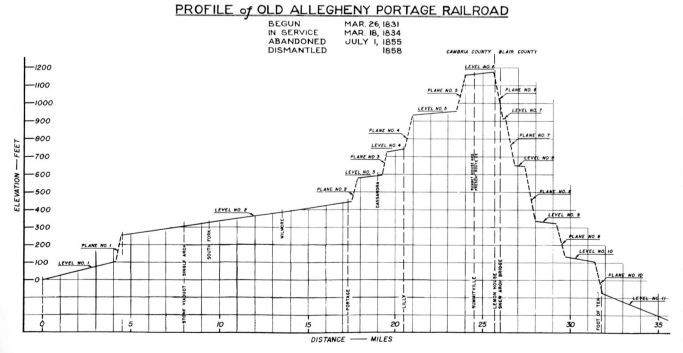

DISTANCE — MILES

George Shaw's realistic paintings show how steam power brought sectionalized boats, *above*, along stretches of Pennsylvania's Main Line Canal, and how canal passengers fared at Lemon House at the summit of the Portage Railroad. *Pennsylvania Historical and Museum Commission photos*

ately rejected the fragile wooden locks that had originally been planned and directed the construction of expensive, exquisitely built stone locks (whose only shortcoming was that the stones were sealed with inadequate mortar). Slightly later replacements of these magnificent locks, whose chambers measured 74 by 12 feet and were 3 feet deep when not filled, may still be seen along the north bank of the river at Little Falls. The originals worked almost perfectly and, in the words of Elkanah Watson, "*doubled* the intrinsic value of the lands and produce on [the route of] these waters." This successful improvement and the Champlain Canal (which went by the name of the Northern Inland Lock Navigation Company) seemed ready to give New York State a regional waterway system that would challenge contemporary developments on the Connecticut and Merrimack rivers, the Delaware and Schuylkill rivers, or anywhere else in the world.

But just as workmen were rolling up their sleeves to hack away at the bypass canal on the lower Mohawk at Cohoes Falls (which would win the sobriquet "Schuyler's Ditch"), word came to the investors of crises among the land speculators. These manifold disasters were, in totality, the crash in which Robert Morris lost everything and was hurled into debtor's prison; he was but one of many who had overextended themselves, with disastrous consequences. Where so recently developers had gazed upon New York as the region of their dreams, they found there now little but bankruptcy and ruin. Improving the Mohawk River was no longer possible for those few local investors who retained anything from the crash.

It appeared that New York—the weather-swept wilderness where ambitious settlers had sought to replace the Iroquois and the Germans and to profit mightily—would remain what it had always been: an undeveloped, undevelopable state whose only real power rested with patroons in plantations along the Hudson or merchants in the city. Ranking a lowly seventh among the thirteen original states by population count, New York seemed incapable of either translating its rocky interior into any kind of economic asset or of leading other states in opening the way west. Such a southern route as Daniel Boone's "Wilderness Road" through the Cumberland Gap in Tennessee or a restored version of General Braddock's road to Pittsburgh from Cumberland, Maryland, would serve to take the nation to its destiny beyond the mountains. And even New York City, despite its magnificent harbor, its shipping links to other lands, and its promise of a Hudson highway to the interior, would perenially remain second-best to Philadelphia with its network of functioning turnpikes and riverways.

Among the small-thinking state politicians who seemed to make it certain that New York State would forever remain in this limited condition was Dutch-descended Martin Van Buren. Son of a taverner in the comfortable, somewhat in-grown community of Kinderhook, he studied law for the main reason that of the two accepted ways for middle-class New Yorkers to earn a respectable living, tavern-owning and lawyering, he preferred the latter. And he became a liberal Republican-Democrat for the equally conservative reason that he and his fellow burghers wished do everything possible to hold their own against the dominating local grandees.

As a Jeffersonian, Van Buren naturally believed that canals were primarily devices by which Federalists like Senator Schuyler sought to make themselves richer. It therefore gave him a degree of pleasure to lead his minority party in the state legislature to achieve the crushing defeat of state aid to the doomed canals to the north and west. Having rallied behind him the legislators and the landowning voters within his anti-Federalist constituency around Albany. Van Buren trusted that this final nail in the coffin of the canal idea would ensure its burial forever. Farmers in the western settlements would just have to patch up their wagons and keep going down their rocky road to market.

Voices from the West

But a yeast was working within the state that was too powerful for even a politician with the skills of Van Buren to repress. The new locks at Little Falls had both facilitated and stimulated the passage of boats up and down the Mohawk River. Although passage from the Hudson into the Mohawk was impossible because of the falls at Cohoes, freight was shipped overland from Albany to Schenectady. Then it was loaded onto mighty "Durham boats"; that had been imported from Pennsylvania for this upriver service. For many decades before 1790, only the most fragile of rafts and small craft carrying no more than 1½ tons had been seen on the river; anything larger could not have been manhandled around Little Falls. But now the Durham boats, carrying 10 tons and more, could make it all the way to the lakes of central New York State. Furthermore, the increase in traffic tended to bring the costs of shipping down. And with that decrease, more and more families opted to migrate West. The riverway was calling the tune for the development of the region.

Furthermore, towns such as Rome and Canandaigua had been laid out and incorporated by 1790. It was no longer accurate in any way to call central New York State a wilderness. Instead, those Yankees who had displaced the "Bush Germans" schemed in their bustling, up-country towns how to turn modest holdings into fortunes. They founded newspapers, wrote prideful letters, took up the reins of politics. They were determined to make their voices heard. Their agitation for an improved transportation system eventually even reached the ears of such leaders as the cabinet members of the new Jefferson administration in Washington and the state power brokers in Albany and New York City.

As the internal improvements promised by Albert Gallatin (Jefferson's Secretary of the Treasury) assumed clearer definition, New Yorkers heard to their horror of the work undertaken on the National Road, from the head of the Potomac to Wheeling on the Ohio. This was apparently viewed by Gallatin and others as the route that should claim primary responsibility for conducting the nation West. Unless rapid action was taken, New York would be outflanked and bypassed; the worst fears of Elkanah Watson would be realized.

Taking up pens, not swords, to fight for their state's share of the federal funds, articulate Yankee-Yorkers also sought to propagandize their neighbors into local political action. A ground swell of support rolled across the state, taking palpable form in the "Canal Ticket" on the ballot of 1807. Both Federalists and Democrat-Republicans, everyone who was in favor of the cross-state waterway, swarmed to this incipient party. A letter-writer to the *Genesee Messenger,* a canal advocate signing himself "Hercules," was undoubtedly the most important contributor to the enthusiasms of the activated audience.

His real name was Jesse Hawley. He had moved to the Genesee Valley from New England around 1800. His series of catalytic letters appeared from October 1807 through April 1808. He deserves credit as first to insist that the western terminal of any state canal had to be on the shores of Lake Erie; because of that concept his writings were greeted in some quarters as "the effusions of a Maniac." Though thoroughly sane, Hawley knew more, in fact, about regional pride and rousing the populace than he did about hydraulic engineering; he favored the construction of an inclined plane along much of the route.

As well as rallying his fellow Yorkers to the cause of a system that would go all the way to Lake Erie, Hawley persuasively condemned private monopolies. Urging the voters of the state to undertake the financial responsibility themselves, he called upon political leaders to introduce legislation that would keep the project free from the wealthy few who sought to undertake such works for their own long-range profit. The leaders of the upstate Democratic-Republican Party responded vigorously to his call, vowing that neither foreign investors nor entrenched aristocrats should benefit from this public-interest work. Indeed, the project should be carried out by the people, for their own benefit.

Among the leaders who then came forth with the wit and vigor to push the concept along to completion were Judge James Geddes of Onondaga (today's Syracuse) and Mayor De Witt Clinton of New York City. Geddes, like Jesse Hawley, represented western interests. Specifically, his interest was salt—the salt that ultimately provided the driving economic force for the Erie Canal's success; the underground dome of salt that had been the secret wealth of the Iroquois. Geddes knew that the only way to handle the salt business profitably was to ship the heavy material inexpensively. That meant by canal. Though a lawyer and no engineer, Geddes had sufficient influence to obtain a commission from the state in 1808 to survey possible routes for the proposed canal. For this report (which he delivered in January 1809) he was to be paid the princely fee of $600. While considering the possibility of a route all the way to Lake Erie, Judge Geddes believed it would be sufficient for the canal to reach Lake Ontario.

Two years later, however, Geddes expanded his horizons and concurred that the system must reach Lake Erie. In that judgment may be seen the growth of the man: having taken up the cause of canals for the rather limited local purpose of facilitating the shipment of salt from his town to the East Coast, he came to see that the region (if not the nation) as a whole should be served by a canal that truly bound East to West. Yet, while deserving credit for the intelligence he put into his researchings (turning himself into perhaps the nation's leading canal engineer in the process), he cannot be given high marks for all of his notions.

For example, the inclined plane that he imagined, a uniform slope that would be constructed all the way from Lake Erie to the ridge between Schenectady and Albany, was absurd. Where this ramp worthy of the Pharaohs crossed the northern end of Lake Cayuga, it would be 130 feet high, based on a cross-lake causeway that would be a mile long; where the monumental plane crossed the mouth of Schoharie Creek, it would be 150 feet high, totally beyond the technology of the day. Fortunately, Judge Geddes was not one to stick stubbornly with a mistaken idea.

The final report of the judge, delivered to the legislature in 1811, was viewed as "disappointing" by the state's canal commissioners—who included such outstanding figures as Gouverneur Morris, Robert Fulton, Robert R. Livingston (the Hudson River baron who financed Fulton's steamboat), and De Witt Clinton. But the report did have enough combined wisdom and imagination to get them thinking.

Van Buren's Conversion

Putting his remarkable talents to the task, De Witt Clinton (who had been brought on board the canal commission) now wrote a stirring document called the "New York Memorial," at the state legislature's request. He took this document on the road, staging a series of stirring speeches across the state. At some points he preached to the already converted, at others to opponents who told Clinton to go home. His oratory proved effective: noting the generally favorable response to Clinton's strategem, the legislature authorized $5 million for the canal.

Undeterred by the imminence of war between the United States and Great Britain, Clinton and his fellow canal commissioners moved deliberately ahead with the project of a canal to Lake Erie. But when the War of 1812 finally broke out, particular havoc swept down upon western New York State. All available funds were exhausted, and the image of a mighty empire here in New York was shattered by unstoppable British raids on Lake Ontario ports. The Yorkers' confidence in themselves recovered only partially after Thomas Macdonough's 1814 victory on Lake Champlain.

Just two years later the legislators were considering the Erie Canal again, focusing on a new bill that would give the canal commission $20,000 seed money to arrange loans, get new funds, and begin land negotiations. The bill was routinely contested by the perennial opponent, Martin Van Buren, though his position now seemed less adamant. Possibly the Democrat-Republicans of the West had impressed him with their dynamism and political strength (and possibly with their determination to get their canal, party or not).

But most believed that Van Buren's opposition to the canal stemmed primarily from his hatred of De Witt Clinton; because of that personal and party hatred, no issue could ever join them. To Van Buren, De Witt Clinton—son of the general and nephew / secretary of former Governor George Clinton (respected as "Father of New York State")—epitomized the moneyed downstate elite. Aged forty-six in 1815 (when Van Buren was thirty-one), De Witt Clinton had by then served as the industrious and respected mayor of New York City for ten terms. He had also served as U.S. senator and state senator and lieutenant governor; in 1812 he had run strongly but unsuccessfully for the presidency against James Madison on an independent ticket attractive to Federalists and Democrats alike.

Because of his advocacy of such causes as abolition from slavery, more voting rights for Roman Catholics, and less severe punishment for indebtedness, Clinton's reputation was that of the aristocratic liberal. And because of his extraordinary appearance—his magnificent head, his titanic physique—Clinton was given the name Magnus Apollo by the press. His intellectual and administrative capabilities were even more extraordinary.

A member of Columbia University's first graduating class, Clinton continued to educate himself in the manner of a Renaissance prince throughout his too-brief life. Natural history—the biology and geology of his native state, particularly along the route of the canal—became the subject he pursued most passionately, especially when he was in the company of one or another of his four sons. By 1810 his knowledgeable advocacy of the canal and his dominance of the canal commission reached the point where the project and the man appeared identical. Clinton owned the Erie Canal; he and that daring concept would fail or succeed together.

And many there were besides Van Buren who plotted the failure of both. The citizens of Schenectady, for example, despised the idea of a canal, for it would cut them out of the lucrative business of transporting goods overland from Albany to the upper level of the Mohawk River through their city's own entrepôt. And in New York City there were numerous opponents. For although Clinton's constituency there remained solid, the city belonged increasingly to the rowdies of Tammany Hall. Clinton and his family had always been opposed to the Federalists (including their federal constitution, preferring the concept of "state sovereignty") and had also steered clear of the grandees along the Hudson. But despite their liberal position on many issues, they had little in common with the radicals, mechanics, and farmers who rallied to Tammany's call and bulked up the Democratic Party. The Clintonians existed as an independent party, proud and somewhat obsolescent.

De Witt Clinton's hold on the loyalties and affections of New York City voters was weakened by an even more insidious factor than his opponent's cleverness: his own personality. Tactless and sarcastic, he governed in a manner too imperious for many to take. For all his honesty and industriousness and belief in the welfare of the people, he could not gladly share the reins of government with any representatives of that people. He knew what the citizens of this somewhat democratic society needed, he felt, and he would bestow it upon them. Would they not cooperate?

In the earliest years of the century, Clinton had not favored the canal idea, seeing such an upstate development as a potential danger to the dominant position of New York City. But, rather like James Geddes, when Clinton understood the beneficial consequences that would befall the entire region, he swiftly reversed himself. It was he who, equipped with Geddes's survey, had gone to Washington with the redoubtable Gouverneur Morris in 1811 in hopes of snaring some federal funds. But, as seen, the Jeffersonians were shy in delivering on their promises of aid for internal improvements. It was at that point, apparently, that Clinton determined that the people of the state should carry out the project on their own—under his leadership.

"The Great Western Canal" was the official name given to the project as it came under scrutiny in the legislative season of 1816. With a promotional, destiny-charged name like that, who could possibly be opposed? Furthermore, it was increasingly possible to produce surveys that were accurate and even scientific. Although the supreme canal-planner, William

Weston, had declined an invitation to undertake that work (presumably because of his suspicions that this canal corporation might collapse out from under him, as had the Western Lock and Navigation Company), the replotting would be competently managed by two typically up-and-coming Yorkers. They were the salt-conscious self-made canal expert Judge James Geddes and another attorney who had also had deep experience with surveying land claims, Judge Benjamin Wright of Rome. These two local legal lights presumed to design the canal's westward route.

As a result of their 1816 survey, an exact picture of the proposed ditch (and of the necessary steps up and down and up to western New York from the Mohawk River) was then put before all interested eyes. To make the bill even more irresistible to the legislators, it was again coupled with a northern canal that would link Lake Champlain with the Hudson. The signs for passage were good. But questions remained about the feasibility of the Erie project, given the state of engineering knowledge at the time and the budget limitations. Martin Van Buren, for one, needed to know whether there existed in America the talents and techniques to construct the proposed locks; he recommended that the Middlesex Canal be thoroughly studied for that purpose and also for purposes of analyzing the financial flow. And so 1816 dragged on and became 1817, with the legislators talking much, deciding little.

Then came two shockingly negative events, with a tremendously positive net impact. The first was a well-intentioned motion introduced on the floor of the U.S. Congress by that great proponent of internal improvements John Calhoun of South Carolina. On March 3, 1817, this craggy southerner—who had earned his "War Hawk" reputation from agitations for the just-concluded, nearly disastrous war with England—introduced a bill that would grant aid to New York's proposed trans-Appalachian canal. He was not alone in seeing this canal as the most important improvement to be attempted on the North American continent; the bill was passed by both the House of Representatives and the Senate with impressive majorities. But swiftly the bill was vetoed by President Madison on grounds of its unconstitutionality—the final action of his not distinguished term in office. This was all strangely reminiscent of President Thomas Jefferson's dismissal of the Erie Canal in the previous decade. What was there about the White House that it so disdained a canal in the North?

Expectant New Yorkers, infuriated by the veto, then received a shock of another kind. One of the Hudson Valley's wealthiest patroons, J. Rutson Van Rensselaer, having concluded from the recent surveys and studies that the projected canal was feasible, declared that he would come forth with much of the needed financing. This assumed, of course, that he would receive a commensurate share of the tolls. So here was this Federalist of the old school, after all the years of agitation in the West for a canal that would be funded by and controlled by the people themselves, choosing to play the role of Riquet on the Canal du Midi: the private monopolist who would ultimately get the cream at the top of the bottle.

The coincidence of these two events was too much, even for Martin Van Buren. Suddenly, to the amazement of legislature observers, he swung his entire bloc of votes behind the measure for the Erie and the Champlain canals. And he proposed, in a master stroke, that construction funds be borrowed, through banks in the region, from the state proper. The work should not be financed by or belong to the wealthy few.

This much-chewed-over bill, introduced in 1816 and carefully reworked in 1817, called for a ditch in the middle of New York State that would be independent of all rivers and would run west only as far as Seneca Lake. The project would continue from there to Lake Erie when and if this first stretch proved its worth. Van Buren's support and the prudent character of the bill combined, at last, to give New York State the canal for which so many had yearned, for which the land and its history seemed specially made. All representatives from New York City had opposed the undertaking, but otherwise the entire state seemed dedicated to it, following the commanding lead of Clinton and vociferous partisans from the West.

Van Buren's last-minute support for the canal was paramountly a political maneuver, like most of his actions; he by no means deserves to be hailed as one of the true "fathers" of the canal. The little giant from Kinderhook used to be portrayed by historians as the prototypical democrat. Thus he would be seen here as the leader who, in finally favoring the canal, heeded the voice of the needful and aroused people. But recent historians see him as more of a manipulator for the sake of power, see his switch to the canal as a typical attempt to turn what the people wanted to his own advantage. For he was not truly interested in such democratic measures as broadening the franchise or financially assisting the people or reforming the ancient mechanisms of state government. He would do only what helped him and his "Albany Regency" or "Holy Alliance" create an unbeatable Democratic machine. Traditional-thinking and petit-bourgeois and limited in his objectives, he stands in contrast to Clinton, visionary and independent and even radical, however autocratic.

Clinton's Dream

Yes, the passage of the bill in 1817 represented mostly a triumph for Clinton, across the state if not in the legislature. It was he above all who had stressed the theme of unity, he who had convinced the state's various regions that they must work together for the complete project. With characteristic wit and sarcasm, he sneered at those who opted to take the canal merely to Lake Ontario, proclaiming that the way to the west could be won only by attaining first Seneca Lake and then Lake Erie, reaching into the heart of the continent. (The real reason for his emphasizing this point so often and so abrasively was not that he was a visionary; he feared that the alternate Ontario connection would encourage western shippers to send their goods by that lake and the St. Lawrence to Canadian ports rather than directly to New York City.) Even though triumphant, De Witt Clinton made enemies even as he won support; he certainly did not hold the power of the state in his hand.

Much of that power belonged, under New York's antiquated constitution, to the so-called Council of Revision. This bizarre body, left over from colonial times, had the authority to review any legislative act. On it sat such eminent personages as James Kent, chief justice of New York's supreme court, and Daniel Tompkins, who was currently serving as Monroe's Vice President. A staunch if not particularly nimble Jeffersonian, Tompkins had once won fame by suspending the state legislature in order to prevent the chartering of a state bank. The members of the council, eight in all, tended to approach the subject of canals with high suspicion. The entire state was being put at risk because of the way the $5 million needed for the canal was to be financed; this appeared to be a huge gamble on an unknown future. Even if one looked at the proposal's strongest argument—-that the canal would serve to transport the region's agricultural surplus to market most advantageously—where, in fact, was that agricultural surplus? Then there was the eternal question of who would really benefit financially as a result of the proposed internal improvement.

These were among the questions raised by Vice President Tompkins when he joined the other council members. He still confessed to be in shock from the damages the state had sustained in the recently concluded War of 1812. Then, having listened like a good politician to the this-way-and-that discussion of the issue, he deduced that his was the critical vote among the evenly split members. And he determined to put his weight against the risky, notional canal.

As the story of that crucial council meeting is told, Tompkins began his negative argument with the intelligence analysis (presumably from sources available to him as Vice President) that the British would never allow the late war to go unavenged. The British, he said, now recognized that their continuing effort to dominate North America could not be successful until the Great Lakes were secured. And that could only be done by letting British regiments loose against forts on both of the New York lakes. As the gentlemen around the table stirred uneasily, Tompkins concluded by declaring that if there was any money in the state treasury to be spent on public assistance, that money should go not to the problematical canal but to the military defense of the region.

But there was something so ponderous, so wiseman-from-Washington, about the Vice President's presentation that the council members were antagonized rather than persuaded. Chancellor Kent, who ultimately cast the swing vote in the meeting, arose. His response to Tompkins concluded: "If we must have war, or have a canal, I am in favor of the canal. And I vote for the bill!" On the basis of that brave if illogical riposte, the legislative bill was formally signed and approved. The canal commissioners could get on with their work; the first shovelful of earth could be dug. And De Witt Clinton—who had been elected governor the preceding fall (1816) on the strength of western votes—could get on with the business of fulfilling his dream.

Chapter Three

THE AMERICANIZATION OF CANAL-BUILDING

THE CANAL CONCEPT, which had been a political issue for so long, plaything of publicists and legislators in the halls of the capital, now became a personal challenge for engineers and contractors in the field. Yet it also remained a highly public matter, with newspapers and pulpits of the day commenting regularly on its progress, its problems, its disruptions of what had been before. And to sociologists and anthropologists of today, looking back, the very grasping of the tools to do the digging here in New York State seems to have changed this species of mankind—as much as when man first shaped a stone into a knife.

Although canal-building had been perfected as a modern process in Europe and had been imported and applied here by Weston and other foreigners, now it would become an intensely, creatively American affair. Furthermore, by cutting their mark so deeply into the land, these New York canal-builders would simultaneously cut themselves free of the old earth-man relationship—for good or ill.

All the nation, with envy or admiration, read the reports and made odds on whether the Yorkers could get it done, and could change themselves thereby. For it was a performance before all eyes, a claim for superiority that was recognized as just that. It was also an invitation to others to come along and participate, be they workers on the project or passers-through. A lyric of the period ran:

> Then there's the State of New York, where some are very rich;
> Themselves and a few others are digging a mighty ditch,
> To render it more easy for us to find the way
> And sail upon the waters to Michiganiay—
> Yea, yea, to Michiganiay.

But it remains for us to see precisely what the personal impact of this technological phenomenon may have been. Did the diggers, the engineers, the commissioners, all leap ahead through adversity and achieve riches and glory? Were they enabled by this work to pursue happiness (as promised in the revolutionary nation's Declaration of Independence) more actively?

Hosannahs, and Boos, in Rome

All America concurred that the greatest excitement of the year 1817 was the turning of the first shovelful for the Erie Canal. That glorious event was staged on July 4, naturally, at Rome, ancient site of Forts Stanwix and Schuyler. More accurately, it was staged about half a mile outside the little village, for that was the way the engineers had decided the ditch should bend, according to the dictates of the gradients. Outraged villagers protested that since the canal spoke to the future of the entire region, it and its business should not go along the outskirts as planned but through the very center of town. They believed, further, that the old canal of 1791 (which had served their community so well) was being unjustly murdered by the new route.

Despite the protests and pretensions of Rome's inhabitants (and despite all the history they and their forebears had experienced here at the head of the Mohawk River), the frontier village seemed no real match for its name. Rome this little village was not. And the words that rolled forth in the dedication speeches as the shovels dug in—the description of a link "between our Mediterranean Sea and the Atlantic Ocean"—seemed equally hyperbolic. Yet hyperbole was in the air and in the minds of these excited people. They cheered with special loudness to one particular phrase: "the vast destinies of these United States." That's what they were about.

With flags flying and these grand concepts before them, the band of overdressed locals and visitors strove to forget all past failures. Everyone spoke as if the completion of the "Great Western" were just around the corner. Had De Witt Clinton not said the first section would be ready for business in two years?

And Rome, though small and prickly, did (if one viewed it from a distance) encourage some optimism. From that summit point, the Hudson was but 100 miles downhill to the east, and the surveyed route to Seneca Falls and the Genesee was about the same distance to the west across relatively level ground. The rest of the way west, the rest of the total 363 miles from the Hudson to Lake Erie, could surely be overcome by the techniques learned in the first phase. It was easy to imagine a time soon at hand when, as one spokesman described it, "by this great highway, unborn millions will easily transport their surplus productions to the shores of the Atlantic, procure their supplies, and hold a useful and profitable intercourse with all the maritime nations of the earth."

By such intercourse, the speaker presumed that the new cities of the region would win sufficient agricultural prosperity and industrial strength to justify, perhaps, the name of Rome and the similarly grand names of other scratched-out villages along the route.

It was the secretary of New York State's Land Board, Robert Harpur, who had dubbed the place Rome. Harpur was "something of a scholar," according to New York historian Carl Carmer; furthermore, Harpur shared the enthusiastic belief that the dream of an empire of classically named capitals could be brought to pass here. His like-minded contemporaries, who succeeded in erasing many of the Iroquois names from the maps and several German names too (searching the atlas for nominations like "Syracuse" and "Utica"), did their work brilliantly. With the new names came a new spirit of ambition and pride, a determination to make a new age of glory happen. Urban renewal experts of today, equally brutal in their disrespect of local history, might take note of this enlivening, neoclassical technique.

Landowners along the route were high with enthusiasm about the

103

future, so much so that they gladly yielded thousands of requested acres to the canal-builders. The giant Holland Land Company—one of those European groups that had leaped in when American speculators had failed to secure the territory after the Revolution—granted more than 100,000 acres for the project. The company's motivation was by no means altruistic; the directors assumed that purchase of remaining land blocks would be stimulated by the new waterway.

Indeed, the Erie Canal may be perceived as essentially a real estate bonanza; certainly there were a number of landowner arrangements that raised eyebrows and enabled that class of New Yorkers to profit extraordinarily. But what's even more impressive is that the farmers of the region, large and small, sought to buy more land for their own agricultural purposes as the canal inched its way across the state: they recognized that they now had a chance to get their increased crops to market cheaply.

De Witt Clinton and his fellow commissioners realized, however, that what had been granted to them by the passage of the bill in 1817 could just as easily be taken away. In a democracy such as New York's (as opposed to a kingdom such as Louis XIV's), any number of imaginable political shifts might occur which could bring the canal foes back to power, and then the funds would be revoked, the dream dashed. The leaders could only hope that enough progress could swiftly be made to impress voters and keep them convinced of the project's value and feasibility.

It was desperately important to get a sizable section of the new, river-independent ditch dug, and to get barges afloat that could freight the salt on which a tax could be charged and carry the passengers and other goods whose shipment would bring forth fees. With these boats passing and revenues flowing, the Canal Fund could be replenished; skeptics might be convinced that the system was functional and extensible. As work progressed steadily from Rome eastward toward Utica and westward toward Syracuse (or actually Salina, where the salt bubbled from the ground), it looked as if one fairly level section could soon be opened. And then what changes might be expected? What kind of great boom times? What temples for Rome?

It must be pointed out that while expectations were high, nothing like the industrial cities of England—indeed, no kind of radical change—was anticipated. The great expectations were directed toward the existent, agricultural economy: let the good business be made even better. Already in 1817 New York was perceived as a one-crop economy, centered about the grain business. Whereas Massachusetts and Rhode Island were surging ahead in the manufacturing of textiles at this time, and whereas Pennsylvania was becoming the dominant power in iron and steel, New York farmers were content with their business of supplying coastal markets with increasing quantities of wheat.

This focus on agriculture naturally determined the look of the land and the character of the population. As late as 1825 (the completion year of the Erie Canal), more than 85 percent of New Yorkers lived in towns of less than three thousand people. In the western counties, large farms sprawled over the distances. And on those scattered farms grew burgeoning families; most of the households contained more than seven chore-sharing children. Even De Witt Clinton, in his most optimistic moments, must have wondered if such a people-scape could produce the labor force for the canal's construction. And where would the engineering skill to build this "miracle" come from?

Digging the Ditch

The first construction contract had been let on June 27, 1817. Farmhands along the route seemed eager to pitch in, volunteering and being volunteered by their bosses as needed. According to historian Ellis, "Most of the contractors were well-to-do farmers who built short sections for agreed sums of money." (As in the case of the Middlesex Canal, an incentive was added to a contractor's basic fee if his section seemed specially difficult.) Laborers were to receive wages as high as 80 cents a day, a tremendous inducement. The word "canal" was on everyone's lips—although, as it was pronounced here, that word sounded like "canawl"; workers were "canawlers." While not many had a clear picture of the hydraulics involved, all could imagine the wondrous day when a surge of brown water would come rushing down the canal bed. In the meantime, the work was well-paid and steady.

It was also brutal. First of all, axmen had to clear a 60-foot swath through the forest, following the surveyors' stakes. Many of the ancient trees to be felled rose 70 feet in the air and measured 20 feet around. After they had crashed to the forest floor, the job was to remove their deep, tangled roots, particularly along the canal bed. Then came the building of the ditch, which was actually a channel dug down between two mounded banks. On one side was the "berm," which was often a kind of dike between the canal and the nearby river. On the other side was the 10-foot-wide towpath.

The task of digging up those roots, moving that earth for mile after mile from dawn to dusk (fourteen hours on a summer's day), six days a week, through a forest fastness that in many places had never been cracked before must have made many a worker hesitate. To modern eyes, this was obviously a mammoth job for only the heaviest kind of equipment—but that was exactly what these workers lacked. Nor, in many cases, did the construction crews have any idea how to get up and over certain recognized obstacles, such as the several broad rivers to be crossed. And that was not to mention the unknown obstacles. To those not caught up in the excitement, the skepticism of early canal opponents continued to seem appropriate. But still the contractors wrestled their ways to solutions, and still the strong men came to do the work.

And as they worked, they sang. History records that the most popular ditty went:

> We're cutting a Ditch through the gravel,
> Through the gravel across the state, by heck!
> We're cutting the Ditch through the gravel
> So the people and the freight can travel,
> Can travel across the state, by heck!

Perhaps they were indeed moved to exalt regional transportation needs in such outpourings of enthusiastic stanzas. But this has the sound somehow of later reconstruction; collectors of the songs admit that "no [scholarly] study has yet appeared" which succeeds in separating the on-site work song from the later barroom ballad. Nonetheless, there's no question that workers of this era were singers or that the Erie was worthy of song.

Certain features beyond good pay (and singing companions?) lured workers to the construction camps: three square meals a day and a much-advertised bonus. If everything went well, there'd be a tot of whiskey every two hours. Also, canal workers were liberated from militia duty. Responding to these inducements, 3,500 men were soon at work, armed with the homely tools (axes, shovels, horse-pulled scrapers) that the contractors were obliged to supply.

The camps to which they came consisted of little more than two frame buildings plus a latrine area, banged together in a rude clearing somewhere along the route of the imagined canal. One of the buildings was a barracks for sleeping, the other a shack for cooking and eating. Management provided no mattresses for the two-tiered bunks. Worker preferences varied for slats of this or that wood; the saying went, "Hickory lasts longer but pine sleeps softer." Nor were doors and windows screened; insects swarmed. thus in the second summer of work on the canal, a summer of severe heat after heavy rains, more than a thousand work-exhausted men lay ill from fevers. Hardly a condition for getting out the guitar.

Yet at first no shortage of workers was reported in the work camps. And though the conditions deteriorated somewhat in the later years of construction (with contractors declining to improve the sanitation qualities of the camps, even in the face of epidemics), the initial attempt had been to give the workers adequate and humane living places. In the typical work camp, the cook served breakfast soon after wake-up call at half an hour before sunrise. Fried mush with maple syrup, or mush and milk, was the staple of this first meal of the day. But big-breakfasting workers also called for quantities of eggs, steak, sausage, pork chops, or ham, supplemented by corn bread, potatoes, and rolls, and washed down by coffee, tea, or buttermilk.

At midday the kitchen crew carried out lunch in wagons to the worksite. Like breakfast, this meal featured quantities of meat and breads. Supper, laid out on the table shortly before sundown, was another hearty feast, from the best that the land had to offer. Such local game as venison and fowl and bear meat—which might seem to us special incentives—struck these workers as poor substitutes for beef and mutton. They insisted that the contractors serve up local fare no more than once or twice a week.

Though local farmhands filled contractors' needs in the opening stages of construction, recruiters were eventually engaged to bring in additional men. They succeeded in finding vast numbers of unemployed workmen, immigrants from abroad, and ex-slaves. It seems not coincidental that the abolition of slave-trading in New York State occurred in the very year of the canal's beginning (1817), by which time that wretched trade was deemed no longer profitable in the North. There were then as many as ten thousand slaves in the state, black and white; total freedom of all was not accomplished until 1827.

The Irish laborers on the canal—often "greenhorns" hustled by recruiters to the worksite immediately after landing—found themselves plunged into a rough world where their muscle was respected but not their religion. They responded with toughness and pluck. But the story that Irish muscle built the Erie Canal almost unaided by others is a false myth. As historians count the numbers, Irish immigration did not reach significant proportions until the 1830s. In the first decades of the century, foreign laborers tended to be British and German. To them, as to all Europeans, the wages offered in New York State (which eventually rose to $1 a day) seemed enormous, more than three times what unskilled laborers could make in the old country.

Whatever the Irish laborers' numbers might have been alongside those of other immigrants (possibly a quarter of the work force), there's no doubt that the Irish did make a distinctive contribution to "Clinton's Ditch." Still-discoverable gravestones, many dating from the later years of the canal's construction, attest to Irish life and death here. So do remembered tales of the ethnic warfare that was the disgrace of the work camps.

The weapon favored by the Irish canallers in those fights is recalled in one of the verses from another well-known ballad, "Paddy on the Canal":

> I learned for to be very handy;
> To use both the shovel and spade;
> I learned the whole art of canalling:
> I think it an excellent trade.
> I learned for to be very handy,
> Although I was not very tall,
> I could handle the "sprig of Shillelah,"
> With the best man on the canal.

Remembered by such ballads, Paddy and his ilk quite readily became the stuff of legends true and false—valuable touchstones for a new nation.

The Engineers and the Challenge

The assembled workers were called upon to produce in mud and mortar a design that had been drafted by an all-American (in fact, all–New York) cast of self-made engineers. As previously mentioned, the central section from Rome to Seneca Lake was given to Benjamin Wright of Syracuse, who, for his achievements on the canal, earned the title "Father of American Engineering." And the westernmost section (to which much creative thought still had to be devoted) was given to James Geddes, who, fortunately, had abandoned his initial fantasy of an immense inclined plane. Geddes soon assigned William Peacock to begin investigating ways of getting the canal over the Genesee River in the neighborhood of Rochester. The easternmost section was handled by Charles C. Broadhead.

It had been the decision of the commissioners and their team of engineers to instruct the diggers to begin "both ways to oncet"—that is, in Yorker parlance, to start off in the two directions simultaneously. They had also made the basic model for the canal's cross section: sloping sides would contain a waterway that measured 40 feet across at the surface and 28 feet at the bottom; the standard depth would be a mere 4 feet. Another decision was that whereas work on the individual segments of the waterway was the responsibility of the respective contractors, the state would take responsibility for the eighty-three locks that would be needed along the canal's entire 636-mile length (twenty-seven of them in the first 15 miles up around the falls at Cohoes) and for the several aqueducts.

Each of the eighty-three locks was to carry a boat up or down an 8-foot step. That extraordinary number of locks was needed because although the difference in altitude between the Hudson River's surface and that of Lake Erie was and is only 568 feet, the engineers had to plan descents into broad valleys as well as ascents over further summits along the canal's route. After the climb to the Rome level, a westbound boat was taken down from Syracuse to the level of Lake Onondaga; then, after climbing back up to the previous level again, the boat descended toward Seneca Falls. But from there, it was all uphill to Rochester and Buffalo—a vertical distance for the total passage of 688 feet.

As a result of the route's ups and downs, the supply of water to the canal (and the drainage of excess water from the canal in flood times) was far trickier than it would have been if a single slope had existed, downhill from Lake Erie. To keep the water flowing gently (eastward most of the time) into and along the canal's level stretches, engineers had to construct an elaborate system of feeders for the different segments. These feeders reached far into the mountainous regions on either side of the route, tapping high lakes and dammed streams. A secondary purpose of the feeders was to allow canalboats to reach—as soon as possible—such key shipping sites as Salina, where the salt was processed. To handle any excess water, the engineers planned a series of sluices and "waste gates" that would, they hoped, regulate the water level in the canal.

Then there was the dreaded problem of conveying the east-west canal across such north-south-running streams as Schoharie Creek, Chittenango Creek, and the formidable Genesee River (as well as the Irondequoit valley). At Schoharie Crossing—an ancient site from the French and Indian Wars era, known then as Fort Hunter—the engineers attempted an ingenious but not quite workable solution. The creek was blocked and controlled by a 650-foot-long dam, creating a pond into which canalboats were admitted through guard locks; then the boats were to cross the pond and continue on, through another lock, to the canal. But the Schoharie proved too strong to be tamed by this fragile system; in one of the first enlargements of the Erie Canal (1840), the dam-crossing was replaced by a handsome multiarched aqueduct, whose ruins may still be seen. At the Genesee, an aqueduct some 802 feet in length was deemed the only solution. The construction of this magnificent "waterbridge" with its eleven Roman-style arches proved so demanding that it almost jeopardized the on-time completion of the politically crucial first section.

The Mohawk River itself had to be crossed at two awkward points where the bends of the river dictated that the canal must be moved to the other side. At these points and in other narrow passageways where there was hardly room for both the riverway and the canal between the shoulders of flanking mountains, engineers had to build aqueducts whose bases sometimes rested on the riverbed. The aqueduct-lofted canal (which had to be positioned high enough above the river's surface to escape the frequent floods and seasonal high water) sometimes seemed to hang out over the river, if contemporary drawings are to be believed. Here and elsewhere the builders of the Erie went through the same process as on the Middlesex: inexpensive and swiftly built wooden aqueducts failed and fell apart, needing to be replaced by far more expensive and time-consuming masonry constructions.

By Powder and Cement

The builders of the Erie Canal also faced the twin difficulties of earthen banks that would leak and rock faces that would resist the simple picks and shovels that the laborers brought to the job. But against the latter difficulty, contractors could now aim an improved weapon: Du Pont blasting powder. The United States was fortunate in having become the home of this rich French family whose father and sons had exiled themselves, in a very calculated way, from their native land after the tragedy (as they saw it) of the French Revolution. In America the Du Ponts found a grand opportunity to establish a family corporation that would focus its products at and derive its wealth from the very primitiveness of the land. What was needed here most of all was dependable black powder, powder effective enough to reshape the continent. They would perfect and supply that product.

Son Irénée Du Pont returned to France after the family's arrival on American shores (where they had entered, originally and unsuccessfully, into the land development business) to renew studies at the laboratories of his former master, Antoine Lavoisier, the father of modern chemistry, who had been executed during the French Revolution. There he studied not only the science of combustion but also the process of grinding and measuring the essential ingredients until the mixture was exactly right. Those ingredients are—and had been known to be since the thirteenth century—saltpeter, sulfur, and charcoal.

Then, having returned to America, Irénée Du Pont searched the mid-Atlantic states for the best site for his powder mills, a site that would have advantages for both manufacturing, by waterpower, and distribution, by water. This was located on the swiftly falling, rarely failing Brandywine River in Delaware. And from the uniquely designed stone-walled mills there the Du Ponts began to produce in 1802 America's first scientifically manufactured black powder.

The family's investment seemed risky at first, given the slow pace of American development. But, aided by the needs of the War of 1812 and

111

the demands thereafter, the Du Pont enterprise prospered, because of both the excellence of the product and the skill with which it was promoted across the land. That skill was sufficiently dazzling so that many writers, even historians who should know better, are often heard to say that the Du Ponts aided American development, and the Erie Canal in particular, by producing a new type of gunpowder. It was not new at all, it was the same black powder (polished or unpolished) that had sputtered and exploded erratically for centuries; but now, in the Du Pont packaging, it behaved in dependable ways. And because of that dependability, the men who used it on the Erie were quantum leaps ahead of the canal-builders who preceded them.

For the other ancient difficulty of leaking earthen banks, the Yorker builders could do nothing but learn how to puddle, along with all the European builders before them. But for the closely related difficulty of sealing the joints of stone locks with waterproof cement, a local solution revealed itself almost miraculously. Or perhaps this solution should be viewed as one of those several notable American inventions that were stimulated by the intense pressure of the Erie Canal. It had to be built, and made to work, fast enough to inspire confidence.

The builders of the Middlesex Canal had made up for the lack of hydraulic cement by importing "trass" from the West Indies, but that East Coast solution was not practical for the construction chiefs in upper New York State. The story of the discovery of a suitable local material near the canal begins with a young would-be engineer named Canvass White. Typically for this region, young White had been born of a Yankee-immigrant family, in Whitestone, New York; also typically, he was well educated and interested in matters technological. Though not particularly robust, and wounded in the War of 1812, he leaped at the chance to help Benjamin Wright make his 1816 survey of the canal route. As he fulfilled his part of that rugged assignment in the field, he must have wondered with every step how all those necessary locks could be built and mortared to hold water in time and on budget.

The next year, when Canvass White was twenty-seven, he submitted a proposal to De Witt Clinton and Benjamin Wright that he be authorized to go to England, at his own expense, and investigate the famous canals of that industrialized nation. He wanted to become intimately familiar with how they worked, down to the last detail. His wish was granted. Soon, at the beginning of 1818, he was writing home to his father that, on foot, he had "traveled 400 miles [which would soon be extended to 2,000], passed through a number of tunnels and over several aqueducts. . . . One aqueduct . . . consists of nineteen arches of cast iron." His notebook rapidly filled up with canal specifications and techniques; his mind struggled to adapt them to the New York scene. In much the same manner as Thomas Jefferson and Elkanah Watson, he was more interested in the usefulness at home of what he was discovering than in the sights themselves.

But upon returning home, White found to his distress that the canal commissioners were already threatened by the unexpectedly high costs of completing locks on the first section of the canal. The highest item in those construction overruns was consistently the hydraulic cement, which had to be imported from Europe.

Then came a report that a Yorker named Mason Harris, a contractor who had undertaken the culverts and aqueducts on the segment between Rome and Salina, was working with an odd variety of limestone that seemed effective in withstanding water pressure. Harris invited officials and other contractors to come and see how, when used in connection with the culverts he had built, this cement would not "slack" (meaning that it would not become diluted or weakened when in contact with water). Canvass White rushed out to Harris's home in Madison County, south of Rome's Oneida County, to investigate. There he found that this peculiar kind of limestone, when put in water, did the opposite of slacking—it became more solid.

A dramatic picture of Canvass White's excited discovery of the new material has been painted by canal historian Noble Whitford (working from White's notes). When White arrived in Mason Harris's hometown of Chittenango, he went immediately to a trip-hammer shop where he'd been told Harris was going to demonstrate the strange behavior of his limestone in a series of experiments. He watched as Mason pulverized the stone and burned it and mixed it with sand in the traditional manner. Then, as part of the experiment, the dry mixture was "placed in a bucket of water for the night. In the morning it had set, was solid enough to roll across the floor, and by Dr. Barto [a scientific gentleman from Herkimer

County] pronounced *cement,* not inferior to the Roman of Puteoli or the Dutch Tarras of the Rhine."

Canvass White then devoted himself to the mining, analyzing, and proper mixing of this superior limestone from Chittenango. And because he carried out that work so ingeniously and productively (all at his own expense) for the benefit of the canal-builders, it could well be said that he "invented" New York's own form of hydraulic cement. He then put his brother in charge of the operation, never receiving adequate compensation for his dedicated work. In the words of Benjamin Wright, the young man (who died in 1834, aged forty-four) gave "an incalculable benefit to the State." His cement was surely one prime reason why the canal's locks and culverts were solidly built and the entire project did not break the construction budget.

Another reason why the canal could be built despite the natural hazards and the primitiveness of the equipment was that other men, on lower levels of employment than Canvass White, were equally inventive. The most dramatic example of this indigenous creativity was a gigantic stump puller so powerful and efficient that it allowed a team of horses and seven men to "grub" forty stumps a day. The dimensions of this super winch stagger the imagination. The shaft of the axle was 30 feet long and 20 inches in diameter; at either end were wheels 16 feet in diameter by which it was rolled into place; positioned midway along the axle was a third wheel 14 feet in diameter. When the destination for stump-pulling had been reached and the outer wheels chocked, a chain from the stump was secured to the axle shaft; and when the horses (or oxen) hauled on a rope that had been wound around the perimeter of the central wheel, the turning axle pulled up the stump with an ease that seemed, again, magical. It was, of course, the down-gear advantage of the 14-foot wheel over the axle shaft's 20 inches that gave the winch such power.

Another wonderful invention was a kind of endless screw that was used to bring down the massive, unbending oak trees. A cable from the tree was wound around a drum that was made to revolve by this screw, or worm gear. When the screw was turned by a crank, grooves along its length engaged teeth on the drum's axle; the drum revolved, the cable pulled, and the tree was bent inexorably down and snapped short. All by the power of one man's arm. There were also such helpful inventions as a plow with an additional cutting blade for ripping up roots, mule-powered wheelbarrows, and scoops for dredging watery earth. On viewing these devices today at the canal museum in Syracuse, one admires both the in-the-field inventors who had the ideas and the in-the-shop mechanics who forged them out of wood and iron.

The First Rush of Water

As a result of such ingenuity on many levels, De Witt Clinton's expectations of opening the first section of the canal—the 96 miles between Syracuse and Utica—before the end of 1819 were nearly fulfilled. The winter which began that year had been so severe and so lengthy that work on the canal could not start until June. (This was, of course, an inherent difficulty of building America's trail-blazing, east-west route so far north.) And so it was by the narrowest of squeaks that the first barge sailed upon these canal waters, towed successfully from Rome to Utica in one astonishing day, October 22.

A number of days before that, the first surge of water had rushed down the channel. A Utica gentleman confessed to the *Albany Daily Advertiser* that he counted it among the "privileges of [his] life" to have witnessed the scene. Further:

. . . from one of the slight and airy bridges which crossed [the channel] I had a sight that could not but excite and exhilarate the mind. The waters were rushing in from the westward and coming down their untried channel toward the sea. . . . You might see the people running across the fields, climbing on trees and fences, and crowding the bank of the canal to gaze upon the welcome sight.

The pioneer barge to Utica was named the *Chief Engineer of Rome,* in honor of James Geddes, for it was he who had here made the waters run. But it was De Witt Clinton who realized most deeply the political importance of getting the revenues flowing.

He was, therefore, most anxious about the next critical event: the opening of the golden link from Syracuse to Salina. With this accomplished and at the end of that first year of the central section's operations, $5,244.34 was collected as tolls and salt taxes. To that was added the $450.56 taken in at the Little Falls Locks—the old locks, which were still being used at this time by bargemen who chose to go on downstream from Utica in the Mohawk River. These few but important thousand dollars went a long way toward convincing the public that the canal was viable and should be extended in both directions.

An even more impressive argument advanced by Clinton in the cause of continuation was the outstanding performance of the canal-builders in respect to the budget: they had exceeded the estimate of $1,021,851 by little more than 10 percent. Most observers had expected overruns far greater than that, particularly when such changes were made in the original specifications as that the berm-side embankment of the ditch had to be widened from 5 to 8 feet and that wooden aqueducts needed to be torn down and replaced in stone. Also, many additions had been made to the original specifications, including a number of waste weirs that had not originally been recognized as needed. Despite those substitutions and additions, Geddes and Wright and their builders had used sufficient ingenuity and persistence on the job to keep costs rigorously down, to the distress of opponents, who had been sure that the canal would drown itself in a flood of red ink.

But as Clinton and his fellow commissioners pleaded for the go-ahead signal for the remaining sections (and the funds to go with it), they faced a new amalgamation of opponents. These were mostly eastern New Yorkers who trembled at the thought of plunging the state $8 million into debt, mostly for the sake of those aggressive frontiersmen. They pointed out that only the easiest part of the ditch had been dug; expenses would soar at the tough spots!

The easterners then approached Clinton with a bargain: they would agree to the completion of the canal from *Utica* to the Hudson if he and the others would abandon the idea of the final link to Lake Erie. Clinton roared forth his contempt for this unworthy compromise and cajoled the legislators (on the basis of state pride and the prospect of increased revenues from a total system) into passing the bill; he cared little whom he alienated in the process.

Clinton's greatest mistake in these bargaining sessions was to promise with customary force that the whole system would be completed by 1823. That promise—which he would have cause to regret—could only have been made by someone with a sublime sense of his own invincibility or a total ignorance of the difficulties that lay ahead. Ignorant he never was. Winning the governor's race in 1820 by a slim margin, Clinton set out to wrestle his grand work to completion.

Through Swamp and Rock, by Heck

In a swampy area near the outlet of Lake Cayuga, canal construction workers now faced their most frustrating challenge, a stretch of unforgettably hellish digging. Here the route of the canal crossed the Montezuma Marshes, named for a ramshackle village that stood at their edge. Here the rushes grew far taller than a man; the mud was too oozy to prevent that man from sinking in. At first the digging and scooping seemed easy enough, once a standing point was secured. But on return to the same digging site the next day, workers would find the channel no longer there; the sides would simply have slipped back into their original form. So, again, on-site ingenuity was called for: wooden retaining walls at the sides were set up, held in place by stakes driven down deeply into the clay beneath the ooze; the mud from the ditch was shoveled up and over these walls, there to be pressed down into solid embankments.

But as this work went forward, the men were assailed by bloodsucking leeches, by mosquitoes, by turtles and snakes (often killed and worn around the neck as "Montezuma necklaces"). Of all these threats, the most lethal was the mosquitoes; as the summer of 1820 heated up, squads of anopheles swarmed in to deliver their deadly cargo of malaria. The number of men incapacitated by chills or fevers was so high that survivors suspected that the camps themselves must breed the disease; hundreds left the canal for healthier sites.

The desperate doctors, who contended against the sickness with no knowledge of its cause or treatment, tried everything from smudge pots to bleeding. They had a bit of luck on the prevention front with some local gunk known as "Seneca Oil"—petroleum, we would call it. But the only effective medicine seemed to be a strange new drug from Peru, "Jesuit's Bark." The doctors had no way of knowing that this mysterious bark contained quinine, now recognized as the best treatment for malaria.

But as desperate as the swamp with its attendant critters may have been, the situation at the eastern end of the canal was even more demanding. At Waterford, where the Mohawk and Hudson rivers tumble together, the engineers determined that a "flight" of sixteen stairlike locks needed to be built. Such an accomplishment, planning and building a series of locks virtually on top of each other, was a tribute to the dedication and innovative capabilities of the builders. Yet the entire work (including a 1,188-foot aqueduct around the falls at Cohoes and eleven more locks on the way to Schenectady) took so long to design and complete that no barge traffic could move eastward from Schenectady to the Hudson until October 1823. The difficulties surrounding an elaborate new set of locks at Little Falls were also responsible for slowing the pace of completion along this eastward section—demolishing Clinton's promise to have the whole waterway operative by that year.

Clinton realized that he was in political jeopardy. He had just held on to the governorship by a narrow margin in 1820, though the new conservatives (called "Bucktails") had won both houses. His 1822 attempt to stay in power seemed doomed to failure. Not only were the conservatives triumphant and Van Buren in tight control of state politics, but also the people of the state were becoming disillusioned. The astonishing fact that the canal-builders had been able, simultaneously, to complete a canal joining the Hudson with Lake Champlain (as specified in the canal enabling act of 1817) did not help quell the complaints. Where was this promised canal to Lake Erie? It had been a splendid idea, but now, with the eastern section delayed for so long and the western section going nowhere . . . As predicted, Governor Clinton was defeated, replaced by a Robert Yates.

Crises at Lockport and Albany

If a judgment were to be made at this point about what the canal-building process had done for and to the workers themselves, it would certainly be mixed. Though employment was beneficial, hundreds had been killed by accidents and disease. As for the contractors and engineers, though they had scored some successes with in-the-field ingenuity, they had failed to get their job done on time and had proved themselves incapable of solving the truly demanding parts of the task that remained. On the highest level, the canal commissioners and political advocates of the project had fallen totally out of favor. Death, failure, and disgrace seemed to be the human consequences of the Great Western, at least in its construction phase.

Furthermore, the mood of the public was no longer forward-looking and expectant; Bucktails ruled the roost, stressing economies and smaller visions. To be sure, some Yorkers had grown rich as a result of land sales, and farmers were doing better than before. But there was fear that this had been merely a little boom, to be followed by a bust as the reality of a failed dream spread across the land. There was certainly nothing like a "social revolution," the instant effect so broadly claimed by historians of past and recent times. To secure anything like that—as well as for the very completion of the canal—a major miracle now seemed necessary.

Fortunately for the canal, the citizenry, and the career of De Witt Clinton, the right man was ready to make the miracle happen at the western end. His name was Nathan S. Roberts. A typically inventive and ambitious Yankee-Yorker, he had become a large landowner in Madison County. Taking a natural interest in the canal and its potential, he had assisted Benjamin Wright in the surveying of the awkward segment between Rome and Lake Cayuga. In 1818, he'd been appointed "resident engineer" for the construction between Rome and Syracuse. In 1822 he was sent west by the canal commissioners to figure out how the canal might be carried up and over the Niagara Escarpment and on to Lake Erie. He carried with him the destiny not only of the canal but of the entire westward-bent populace of the United States.

Rather than assuming that James Geddes and David Thomas had selected the right location for the locks he'd been assigned to create, Nathan Roberts searched the area with a surveyor's eye and discovered that a declivity in the escarpment somewhat to the east of the planned route was a bit lower, thus easier and less expensive to get up over. There's also the rumor that Roberts fell under the influence of certain landowners in the log-house village nearby which would later become Lockport; the new location made an awful lot of real estate sense to them.

So, back in the spring of 1822, the work had started. Roberts advertised: "1,000 men wanted at Lockport—twelve dollars a month and found." In response, out rushed new bands of eager immigrants, lured by the food and the whiskey, and even by the pay. Their assignment was to chip and blast a 2-mile-long channel out of the 75-foot-high limestone face of the escarpment. It was extremely dangerous work; the flimsy derricks (invented on the spot) frequently dropped stone blocks on workmen in the excavation below. A visiting diarist wrote that in order to protect the village houses from stones that cannonaded out of the blast holes, the buildings "were protected by trunks of trees, about six inches at the butt, and long enough when set around the buildings at about 45 degrees, to meet at the top." Passersby ran for cover when a blast went off.

Roberts's design for the locks was as breathtaking in conception as it was backbreaking in execution. The commissioners, under extreme pressure for completion of the canal, agreed with Roberts that though the plan was expensive, it was both logical and feasible. His design called for two sets of five locks each, one set for upward (westbound), the other for downward (eastbound) traffic; each lock lifted a boat an unprecedented 12 feet vertically—nearly half again as high as the canal's standard locks. Having reached the topmost channel, boats would pass through a deep cleft in the solid rock, one of whose purposes was to admit water from Lake Erie to the rest of the system, down the carefully engineered slope of one inch per mile. The difficult and dangerous work went slowly; more work crews had to be hired. Soon, reversing the earlier work patterns, "two thousand Irishmen were working night and day."

De Witt Clinton, who had revised his promised completion date to 1825, now appeared to be at risk again. Who could believe that the vast quarry at Lockport would ever resolve itself into such a sophisticated pattern of locks? Clinton's enemies, sensing another opportunity to attack him, struck fast—and foolishly. The man himself by this time was nearly exhausted by his labors on all fronts. Enemies charged that he was drinking excessively. But he did everything excessively; biographers agree that though he had had a drinking problem in his younger years, he now was so thoroughly immersed in the canal that all else was pushed aside. His increasing corpulence probably resulted from inability to exercise with his sons (two of whom died early and tragic deaths) and general inattention to himself rather than from any indulgence.

What galled Van Buren's Albany Regency particularly was that despite the fact that they and the Bucktails now controlled the political machinery of New York State (having, more or less, invented that machinery), all eyes in the state and in the nation remained on that man, that artifact, Clinton. As one Van Buren biographer put it, "There was not a newspaper worthy of the name in the Union that did not chart the progress of this titanic undertaking [i.e., *Clinton's* Erie Canal], this symbol of American enterprise, of all that Americans thought promising in their destiny."

And so Van Buren's allies struck, just when the project was at the greatest risk. They also timed their plot to take place when Van Buren himself was off in Washington focusing on the presidential campaign of 1824, so that not even he could interfere with the Brutus-like deed. Flexing their political muscle, members of the Albany Regency instructed the directors of the canal commission to vote Clinton out as president. This the directors obediently did—the maneuver having been led by a particularly unsavory politico named Skinner.

Van Buren, now returned from Washington, was aghast to hear what his supporters had wrought—it could only bring about a counterreaction from the outraged citizens. Summoning Skinner to him, he remarked, "There's such a thing as killing a man too dead." And sure enough, the press and the voice of the public exploded in rage. One state legislator, in deploring the act, demanded of the speaker: "What nefarious and secret design, I ask, is to be effected at the expense of the honor and integrity of this legislature?" And so De Witt Clinton became even more effective in martyrdom than he had been in ordinary working life. The misguided politicians who thought to do him in contributed to the miracle of successful completion by bringing him back onstage.

Celebrations and Farewells

Moving swiftly, Clinton went on to form a new political group called the People's Party. And on that ticket he easily won the gubernatorial contest of 1824. Once again he was in control. Also in control were the engineers and workmen at Lockport—where the challenge caught up everyone in a scene of cooperative endeavor. Townspeople were not to be left out of what benefits the canal might offer: from the 1.5 million cubic yards of excavated rock, they carted away excess stone for the construction of their own houses, and they made zealous plans to take advantage of any excess water for the power of their own industries.

At the center of all this activity now could be seen the amazing two-way locks and the chasm cut through the rock ridge beyond. According to the specifications of the cut, tow mules were expected to tiptoe along a narrow shelf carved into the rock wall some 60 feet above the water's surface—watchful town children were promised an exciting spectacle, as not all mules would make it. By 1824, water had been admitted from the east (that is, from the Rochester side, where the aqueduct across the Genesee River and the challenging levee across the Irondequoit Valley had finally been completed); now that water flowed into a boat basin at Lockport, blasted out of rock at the foot of the locks.

Townspeople then listened with increasing anticipation to reports of how the waterway leading in their direction from Lake Erie and the Niagara River was progressing; they learned that here, in Lockport, would be the meeting place of the eastern and western waters. As the summer of 1825 progressed, they knew with certainty that the canal would be completed by Clinton's second promised date (though the locks were not actually finished until the last second, on October 24). General Lafayette, the peregrinating Revolutionary War hero, had visited the town on June 6 to admire the already famous five-step locks. Not wanting to send him home without the salute he'd expected, canal workers rigged up and set off one of their biggest powder blasts, as if from a cannon. The satisfied general then went on to investigate the canalboat terminus that (after regional warfare with neighboring Black Rock) had been established at Buffalo.

The terminus at the other end of the system, at Albany, had been in operation for some time. Opened with great ceremony in the fall of 1823, it seemed to be almost the hub of the universe, with docks for barges that stretched for miles out into and along the river. Through the gates of the Albany terminus passed barges that had come all the way down from the Lake Champlain canal and were now on their way (after the completion of the Waterford flight) along the Mohawk to the Genesee at Rochester. Also completed, after much debate about proper design, were the three "hydrostatic locks" at Troy, Syracuse, and Rochester. These unique constructions—Greek Revival temples in which officials weighed the water displaced by barges entering the lock—served for decades as the weigh stations along the route, determining tonnage carried and fees charged.

So were death, defeat, and disgrace turned into timely triumph. Failures and mistakes along the way were now perceived as necessary for the lurching advance of America civilization, much having been risked. Even the dead workers were hailed as heroes of the region and the nation. The grand doings of Paddy on the canal were sung in every tavern. As great a poet as Philip Freneau wrote:

> By hearts of oak and hands of toil
> The Spade inverts the rugged soil,
> A work that may remain secure
> While suns exist and Moons endure.

Now an even greater celebration than that for the Albany opening was planned. The bright colors of autumn were reflected in the canal, watered all along its route. From one end of the state to the other now stretched the "shining ribbon of water" (in the words of Samuel Hopkins Adams), the ribbon that tied together coastal ports and interior territories at the heart of the continent. New York, having brought its ends together, could go on to become the Empire State, worthy heir of the Iroquois' Five Nations. New York could now play its key role—in power politics as well as in transportation—of leading the other states toward continental nationhood. Nineteenth-century Americans, fully aware of the major miracle that had happened here, were of a mood to celebrate.

The barrel of flour which used to cost $3 to ship from Rochester to Albany now cost only 75 cents to ship. This one small, central economic fact impelled all the grand excitement. The benefit of that saving spread to anyone who took part in the agricultural scene—which was just about everyone, for there were savings and cost consequences all along the line. Even a raw bale of hay, when carted aboard a barge and floated downstream, could be delivered in the East at a price competitive with local produce. Because of that canal-induced advantage, society stretched and shifted like an awakening giant. In the view of some, now was the time when the social revolution occurred—a revolution discussed in the next chapter.

But the awakened joy behind the celebrations was not exclusively economic. The completion of Clinton's Ditch gave New Yorkers a tremendous increase of self-esteem. It allowed them to believe in themselves, filled them with the kind of moral imperative that Spaniards had felt as their conquistadores claimed the world. One proud New Yorker remarked that his state's engineers and laborers had "built the longest canal, in the least time, with the least experience, for the least money, and to the greatest public benefit." He was sizing up New York's accomplishments, the Americanization of canal-building upon this landscape, against anything that had happened in the world and its history. So let the salutes roar forth!

Ever since midsummer of that promised year of 1825, towns and villages along the way (many of them brand-new creations, with hastily thought-up, hopefully nautical names like Weedsport and Brockport) had been preparing to cheer the first flotilla of officials to pass by on opening day. The prime event on that much-awaited October 26 was the linked firing of cannons all the way up and down the canal's route and even to New York City (500 miles in all), the "echo cannonade," as it was called. First a parade with brass band escorted Governor Clinton and other dignitaries from Buffalo's red-brick courthouse through the town; then with great ceremony their gaudily decorated barge was admitted to the waters of the canal. At that moment (precisely 10:00 A.M.), the lead cannon let fly with its signal blast.

The drill for the cannonade was that gunners in towns along the line would wait until they had heard the roar from the nearest upriver location, then they too would apply bright spark to short fuse. Boom following boom, it took an hour and thirty minutes for the chain of cannonading to reach New York City. After being welcomed there by a massive artillery salute, the cannonade started all over again in reverse up the Hudson and Mohawk valleys—the valleys now echoing blasts of peace and pride, not war and destruction.

Unfortunately, two lads at the village of Weedsport got so carried away by the excitement that they overloaded their cannon for its second blast. The weapon exploded and blew them to bits. "But," historian Carl Carmer reassures us, "their coincidental deaths were not allowed to dull the spirits of the voyagers."

Leading the flotilla of four canalboats was the *Seneca Chief,* with Governor De Witt Clinton standing proudly in the bow. An account of the language used in the exercise staged for Clinton when the flotilla reached Rochester illustrates the heroic mood of the day.

"Who comes there?" an official demanded of the captain of the *Seneca Chief* as he approached the magnificent aqueduct over the Genesee.

"Your brothers from the West on the waters of the Great Lakes," came the well-rehearsed reply.

"By what means have they been diverted so far from their natural course?"

"Through the channel of the great Erie Canal."

"By whose authority and by whom was a work of such magnitude accomplished?"

"By the authority and by the enterprise of the people of the State of New York!"

And that proper answer having been given, "the whole valley of the Genesee shook with the cheering of crowds and the salute of guns and the explosion of fireworks."

If anyone might forget who was the hero of the day, he would be reminded by a prominent decoration on De Witt Clinton's garlanded craft: a huge oil painting of himself as Hercules, now resting from labors. Yet other sights to be seen on board the flotilla gave Magnus Apollo / Hercules competition. On the decks of the next boat, the *Noah's Ark*, crowds could spy a bear, two young deer, a variety of birds (including two eagles), and two young Indians. Also highly visible were two oversized, patriotically painted kegs with water from Lake Erie. In a climax to be known as "The Wedding of the Waters," Clinton would pour these kegs' contents into New York Harbor (along with a mixture of waters from the Mississippi, Columbia, Thames, La Plata, Seine, Rhine, Orinoco, Amazon, Nile, Gambia, Indus, and Ganges rivers). The significance of the completion of the Erie, in the eyes of the spectacle's designers, was worldwide.

But at least it was American. Aboard the *Seneca Chief* with Clinton rode a cargo of potash from the Great Lakes ports of Detroit, Sandusky, Erie, and Buffalo; crates of whitefish from Lake Erie; kegs of flour and butter from Michigan, Ohio, and western New York State; and a special shipment of bird's-eye maple and cedar, ordered by the City of New York for the construction of presentation boxes for the medals that would be struck to honor the occasion. Similarly, the next boat, the *Young Lion of the West,* was piled high with flour, butter, apples, cedar tubs, and wooden pails ("of very excellent workmanship"), some new brooms ("of a superior quality"), and yet another collection of upstate wildlife, including wolves, foxes, and raccoons.

No one at the celebration of the canal and its future commercial benefits raised a painful though abstract question about the historical sacrifices made for this bit of progress: the near-extermination of the Iroquois, the disappearance of the quiet Palatine hamlets, the banishment of the natural wilderness. Forever traffic would unquestionably call the tune, traffic and industry; the industrious and the lucky would become new chiefs of the land.

But there were some who made specific objections to this noisy triumph upon the waters, this apotheosis of Clinton. In Rome (where the citizens were still angry that the canal had not been run through the center of their town) a funeral-like procession solemnly carried a cask of water from the dead old canal to the live new one, and poured it in to mock the "Wedding of the Waters." At Schenectady (where the city fathers continued to regret the fading away of their monopoly of the overland freight business from Albany) the arrival of the official barges was pointedly ignored. Students from Schenectady's Union College were not to be hushed, however; they welcomed the governor and his party to a rip-roaring dinner and a "salute of musketry."

In most towns along the way, the mood remained confident and joyous. After the boats had emerged from one of the long, restful, and scenic water passages to the close-in farms of a rural town, they would be greeted by the ringing of bells and crackling of fireworks; pennants streamed and cheers punctuated the paragraphs of gesturing speakers. At nighttime, the canal towns hung up "transparencies"—illuminated boxes whose cut-out letters hailed CLINTON and INTERNAL IMPROVEMENTS. The day-and-night, week-long journey down the canal must have given even Clinton and his fellow officials the feeling that their dreams of a newly empowered countryside had been fulfilled. The work, the deaths, the disgrace had surely been worthwhile.

Wedding of the Waters

As the official flotilla sailed eastward, more and more canalboats joined in the procession. To them all, the enlarged port of Albany gave a tremendous welcome—and little wonder, for the capital was now the nexus of the Empire State's waterways. After dawn brought a halt to the celebration that had hailed the governor long into the night, two powerful steamboats towed the entire fleet of assembled boats down the Hudson to New York City, where they arrived on November 4. They were met by assembled ships from many nations, prepared to take part in a momentous harbor-tour pageant. "Never before was there such a fleet collected, and so superbly decorated," wrote a journalist with nineteenth-century enthusiasm. "And it is very possible that a display so grand, so beautiful, and we may add sublime, will never again be witnessed."

Then, as whistles tooted and the island-forts' cannons boomed, Clinton reached the end of the harbor, where the waves of the Atlantic could be felt beneath his barge. Here he would order the kegs emptied into the Atlantic, a symbol (in his words) of all that "which has been accomplished between our Mediterranean Sea and the Atlantic Ocean in about eight years." With the action went the prayer that "the God of the Heavens and of the Earth smile most propitiously on this work and render it subservient to the best interests of the human race."

Tears were seen running down Clinton's cheeks. This was, indeed, the moment so long yearned for, the completion. There would be the celebration at City Hall, the welcoming of President John Quincy Adams (accompanied by former Presidents John Adams, Jefferson, Madison, and Monroe), the fireworks and parades. But it was this surging moment in the outer harbor that seemed to hold the most significance for Clinton, this symbolic recognition of the mega-miracle he had accomplished. And one wonders if Clinton, for all his self-confidence and pride, may have considered at this moment how close he had come to having no miracle, no governorship, no triumph at all.

Fortunate was De Witt Clinton to be alive for his great day. He had but a few more years of life in which to enjoy the fruits of his great labors. Like other successful canal-builders before him, he died exhausted, of a heart attack, in 1828, soon after the first commercial barges began to make their ways up and down the waterway. He was fifty-nine.

By then, the state treasurer was receiving more than 8 percent annually on his loan (through the banks) to the canal-builders; the canal had proved itself a solid investment. By 1835 the canal had paid into the state more revenue than the project had originally cost. Furthermore, the canal had increased the value of real estate in New York State by millions of dollars.

127

The glittering waters of the beckoning canal caused increasing thousands to come to the state, to benefit from the dream fulfilled, to have their lives changed forever. As former President Thomas Jefferson put it—without reference to his previous rejection of the project—"This great work will . . . prove to mankind the superior wisdom of employing the resources of industry in works of improvement."

But if the aged agrarian meant to forecast by this that the canal-spawned industries here would learn to direct their profits to public improvement rather than to personal enrichment, he would be proved no prophet. When viewed by people of its day, the Erie Canal seems to have been a mixed blessing. One of the most accurate-sounding reports of how it affected contemporary society exists in the reminiscences of author Samuel Hopkins Adams's grandfather *(Grandfather Stories)*. In one of those stories, one of the main characters, Squire Jerrold, scoffs:

"I'm sickening of the damned canal. . . . There's nothing but worry in it. What does it bring to any locality that it invades? Fever and disease. Lawlessness and rapine and immorality. Conflict between the respectable citizenry and the wild Irish. Corruption of the lower classes and unsettlement of trade."

Another character, a financier, breaks in:

"And money. . . . Don't forget the money, Squire."

Chapter Four

REAPING THE GOLDEN HARVEST

FOLLOWING IN THE FOOTSTEPS of the Marquis de Lafayette, Europeans streamed to New York State to see this new wonder of the New World. There they joined notebook-carrying American sightseers who could not wait to get their canal experiences into print. Traveler Francis Kimball penned one vivid image: "The Erie Canal rubbed Aladin's lamp. America awoke, catching for the first time the wondrous vision of its own dimensions and power."

For although the completion of the canal was an intensely regional affair, with New Yorkers ardently proud of what their own brains and muscle had accomplished, it also inspired enormous national pride. East and West had been united; the young republic now confidently commanded the continent. Never had the national eagle been more popular as a symbol, never had more efforts been made to invent an American style, an American image. This was the time when design-conscious Thomas Jefferson urged that a new American order (possibly the tobacco leaf and the maize sheaf) be created to replace the classical architectural orders. This was also the time when Ralph Waldo Emerson, rejoicing in our new Americanism, wrote:

Our day of dependence, our long apprenticeship to the learning of other lands, draws to a close. The millions that

131

around us are rushing into life cannot always be fed on the sere remains of foreign harvests. Events and actions arise, that must be sung. . . . There are creative manners, there are creative actions and creative words . . . indicative of no custom or authority, but springing spontaneous from the mind's own sense of good and fair.

It was here, along these New York riverways, where the canal had been built upon the well-worn Yankee route west, that the new, nationalistic architecture (strangely called "Greek Revival") would have its most creative flowering. Was it also here that Americans would create, with their revolutionized, nation-conscious spirit, a democratic society which was "good and fair"?

One of the curious reporters who flocked to the Erie, noticing that the canal route was becoming "lined with the rustic parthenons" of the Classic Revival style, opined that a new Periclean Age had arrived in upstate New York. The era's hottest stage sensation, Fanny Kemble, called the canal "beautiful from beginning to end." Perhaps it would be that here, in this region so long fought-over, so miracuously strengthened by a new technology, a different kind of balance could be achieved between the natural world and the mechanistic works of man. Perhaps. Unfortunately none of the enthusiastic note-takers (the "d——d mob of scribbling women," as Nathaniel Hawthorne called them) stooped to peer beneath the natural and man-made beauties and gauge the depth of the disruption caused by Clinton's finally completed ditch.

Canal-reduced shipping costs and increased farm profits had been, as mentioned, the sparks that caused the economic explosion. Whereas the astonishingly industrious town of Rochester had had but four mills in the first decades of the 1800s and had shipped its "Genesee Flour" down the Susquehanna to Baltimore, that pattern soon changed. After the completion of the Erie Canal (when the town's mills, now numbering fifteen, soon to be twenty, consumed more than 15,000 bushels of wheat and produced 3,000 barrels of flour during each twenty-four-hour day), Rochester was sending those thousands of barrels eastward along the Grand Western Canal and southward down the Hudson. Fortunate New York City became, in effect, the Atlantic Coast port of the Midwest. At the other end of the canal, fortunate Buffalo replaced New Orleans as the busiest forwarder of products from the interior.

Other cities also boomed, the people uniting in wealth-producing enterprises. In energized Utica, William Cullen Bryant observed how "the impetus of the city" was derived directly from the canal. In Syracuse, where citizens sought to capitalize massively on the inexhaustible salt springs at nearby Salina, a newly arrived visitor made this quick note: "Every man moved as though he had just heard that his house was on fire." Although the actual builders of the canal in the preceding decades had had to go through misery and failure before they could pull a triumph out of the fire, perhaps now the fullness of the promised harvest would be realized by all—as a result of canal-facilitated businesses and canal-watered industries. Charles and Mary Beard, trying to portray the excited expectations of this time and place in *The Rise of American Civilization,* wrote: "Men who were poor one day were millionaires the next; women who did the family washing on Monday moved into palaces on Wednesday and rode to church on Sunday in carriages."

Many commented on the lust for money, the heightened materialism of these canalside strivers. In contrast to the New England communities they or their parents had left behind, the instant towns and rising cities of these Yankee-Yorkers seemed brash, ostentatious. But at the same time, a kind of rough-and-tumble democracy came into existence, free of the ancient formalities and limitations of the East. When de Tocqueville came out this way a decade or so later, he found suddenly sprung here the new middle class—exactly what he had hoped to find. An Englishman named James Stuart rejoiced to have discovered here "utter democracy"; Samuel Eliot Morison, in writing his *History of the American People,* devoted a central chapter to "The Empire State, Citadel of Democracy."

There was also here a surge of native religiosity. The canal region, once referred to as "the burned-over district" because of fiery revivals in its history, now developed an important new kind of spirituality. What a seeming contrast: the show-off capitalists with their Greek Revival mansions and the Christian enthusiasts with their mass-attendance prayer meetings. Yet, as pointed out in the preceding chapter, these Yankee-Yorkers and their parents had come not from the established (meaning Congregational and Anglican and Unitarian) enclaves of American Christendom; they were hill people, tuned to a more individual kind of revelation. Furthermore, anthropologists have posited that in times of stress

133

and disruption—such as in this time of the building and flowering of the Erie Canal—human societies tend to repair to fundamental spiritual themes. Separated from the more sophisticated, intellectual congregations, men and women strain to catch the songs of original angels.

A popular publication of the day was entitled *The Book of Wealth, in Which It Is Proved from the Bible That It Is the Duty of Every Man to Become Rich.* As might be expected from that attitude and in this period of American culture, get-rich-quickism was accompanied by excessive, brutal exploitation of workers, human and animal. The new rich were under no compulsion to be humane. Samuel Hopkins Adams wrote that for many years it was assumed in his part of Rochester that only the working class could catch cholera or malaria. The death and dying of Irish "bog-trotters" were of little concern to upwardly striving, religious citizens.

Nor was it expected that working stiffs would share in the wealth that was pouring into the cupped hands of the rich and the new middle class. During the eight-year construction of the canal, wages for common laborers had risen above the standard 75 cents a day. Indeed, wages had reached $1 a day ("a good man's pay"), and by the 1840s, they would attain $1.25. But this was still no adequate owner's share of the dynamo that the workers had built. In the judgment of a contemporary New England critic, New York's suddenly arisen capitalists were enjoying fortunes that the Erie Canal and the water-dependent industries had generated, and that they themselves had not made: "Colossal productivity had created a new class, which amassed wealth without creating it."

And of course that new class of wealth tended to forget where it had come from. A historian of Rochester commented a few generations ago: "There may be some who scoff at those who operate canals as plebeian. Yet it was by the little, thirty-ton barge drawing less than two feet of water that greatness and prosperity were born to the Empire State." It was precisely because the new society was plebeian-derived that it had such potential.

This was also the place and time for a reform of state party politics—leading to "people's constitutions," carrying on the political constructions of Van Buren (who continued to object to universal white male suffrage). Whereas Virginia had led the way to broader democracy at the time of the fight for the Constitution, now New York (in the opinion of James McGregor Burns) took on that leadership role. Nonetheless those gains were definitely for the new middle class, not for the workers. They did not have the clout to take possession of the world they had built. In looking at the commanding position of the new rich with their bank papers and stock certificates, a wise spokesman named John Taylor of Caroline explained the phenomenon this way: "We farmers and mechanics have been political slaves in all countries . . . because we are political fools."

Slaves? That terrible word was also used by a contemporary, radical spokesman from New York on the floor of the U.S. Congress. Successful Tammany opponent Mike Walsh declared: "The only difference between the negro slave of the South and the white wage slave of the North is that the one has a master without asking for him, and the other has to beg for the privilege of becoming a slave."

Yet to those of us looking today at this brilliant, potent society, the master-slave formula seems suspiciously facile. There was obviously too much creativity at all levels (economic, religious, political, as well as social) for any such restrictive pattern to control it. These were the people who, at this time and place, did indeed invent the American middle class—with all of its virtues and weaknesses. These were also our forefathers and foremothers. It therefore seems wise to look more carefully at them and how they regarded themselves, dupes or saints or simply lucky stiffs.

Serfs and Canallers

Jesse Hawley, the canal's original booster, boasted, "No single act, no public measure (except the Declaration of Independence and the formation of the United States Constitution), has done so much to promote public prosperity as the Erie Canal." And he was undoubtedly right about the prosperity of one of the two categories of New Yorkers—the speculating townspeople and the entrepreneurial travelers. But what about the men and women who worked to make the canal function—the canallers (pronounced, as explained, "canawlers")? They should be reevaluated in the light of De Witt Clinton's desire to bring about the "modernization of New York society."

By "modernization" Clinton meant that he hoped to advance all people of the region into the new industrial age. So did the canallers really become modernized, as industrial functionaries? This assumes that we retain some respect for those nineteenth-century apostles of progress who sincerely believed that advancement into the new age of industry and improved agriculture would bring unalloyed benefits—a theory not totally destroyed by the recent realization that the benefits were spotty. This realization burst upon us with full force in the disillusioned 1930s, when Charles and Mary Beard wrote: "Whether the Industrial Revolution increased the relative amount of poverty or not, it made the position of mere wage workers more precarious than that of the serf or the farmer; and it concentrated poverty-stricken persons in urban masses. . . ."

At first, industrialized "masses" would not seem any more appropriate a term for the canallers than "slaves." But consider: by the time of the Great Western's completion, some 3,500 men were on the rolls as laborers; twenty years later (1845), there were an estimated 25,000 men and boys working at various tasks along the system. And that omits the women and girls who served as cooks and companions, boat-steerers and purse-keepers. Some New England visitors who did peer into life aboard the canalboats were shocked equally at the mores and the importance of these canalling women, writing that they were "on the whole less educated, more superstitious, and more zealous than the men." Counting them (as one definitely must), this was one huge and throbbing mass industry.

When the captain of the corporation-owned or self-owned barge did not have a wife to run the galley and assist him as steersman, he either had to do it himself or find a willing woman. Beyond that crew member, there were the mule-tender and a boy—called a "hoggee"—who shared the mule-tender's tasks. Although the canal operated only by day when it was first opened, success and heavy traffic soon demanded that the barges be allowed to run at night too. So hoggee and mule-tender worked six hours on, six hours off for the whole twenty-four-hour day, rain or shine, snow or heat.

Mules set the pace both for progress along the canal (usually 2 miles an hour westward, 3 eastward) and for bargers' daily routine. The two teams were switched at 7:00 A.M. and 1:00 P.M., 7:00 P.M. and 1:00 A.M., a process which generally took about fifteen minutes for well-practiced hands. Switch times were also mealtimes, with the cook expected to have hot vittles for all except the mules. Horses had been tried at various times as work partners along the towpath, but mules were found to be the more intelligent, least skittish tow animals.

As the Erie Canal was successively enlarged before the Civil War, heavier barges could travel its length—requiring increased tow power. Hence the invention of three-mule rigs, *above,* at one end of a long towline. *Erie Canal Museum*

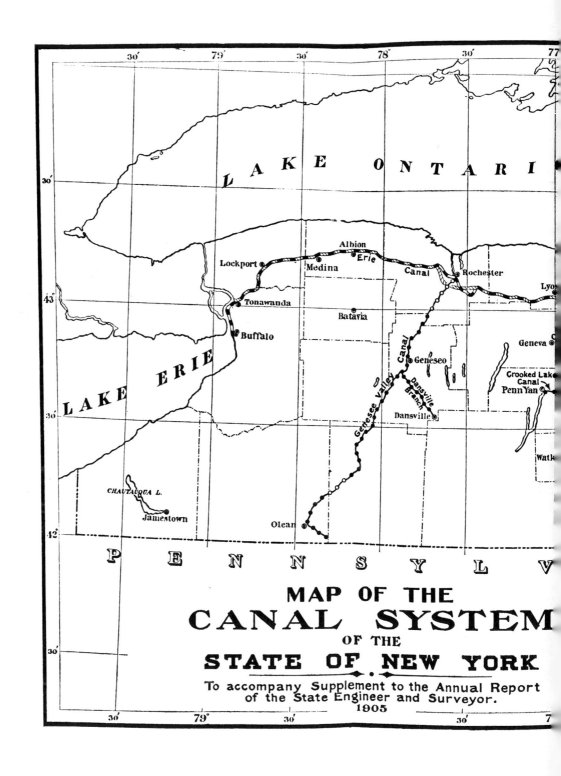

MAP OF THE
CANAL SYSTEM
OF THE
STATE OF NEW YORK
To accompany Supplement to the Annual Report
of the State Engineer and Surveyor.
1905

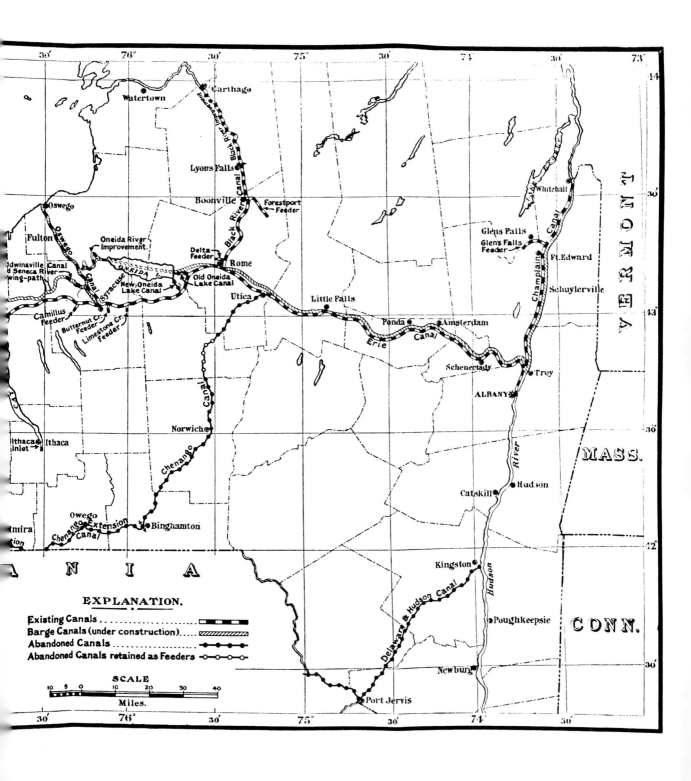

EXPLANATION.

Existing Canals..........................
Barge Canals (under construction).....
Abandoned Canals.....................
Abandoned Canals retained as Feeders

SCALE
10 5 0   10   20   30   40
Miles.

At left, steam-driven lake boats brought Midwest grain to prosperous Buffalo, the Erie Canal's western terminus. *Erie Canal Museum*

Below, in 1880, when many freight vessels were sail-powered and mules still plodded towpaths, the first steam canal boat docked at Buffalo's Central Wharf. *Erie Canal Museum*

Enlarged to handle heavier barges, the aqueduct across the Genesee River at Rochester remains an Erie Canal monument. *Erie Canal Museum*

On the facing page: The first city "revolutionized" by the Erie Canal's impact, Syracuse in the 1870s had shacks for salt-workers, *above,* and mansions for James Street millionaires, *below. Erie Canal Museum photos*

With the canal an integral part of the city's structure, Syracusans could enjoy the spectacle of an 1875 hot air balloon launch in Clinton Square from either barge or bank. *Erie Canal Museum*

In the mid-1800s, construction techniques slowly improved. Horses dragged blocks by cart on rails to the Black River Canal's locks at Boonville. *Erie Canal Museum*

On the facing page: By early 1900s, when the Erie was rebuilt as the New York State Barge Canal, technology included powerful dredges like the *Palmyra, above,* and the "orange peel" dredge shovel, *below. Erie Canal Museum photos*

During construction of the New York State Barge Canal, Lockport's famous set of five double locks (barely visible at far right in photo above) was replaced by two much larger locks with massive steel gates, *center. Erie Canal Museum*

On the facing page: Above, the most important alteration of the Barge Canal was siting it in river beds, where guard gates and other modern systems controlled hydraulic flow. Freighters like the West Kebar, *below,* carried grain on the Barge Canal until the rival St. Lawrence Seaway took over in 1959. *Erie Canal Museum photos*

Handsome structures at typical locks today: Italianate towers, *above,* house power plants; in lesser shelters, *below,* lock tenders operate levers and valves. *Russell Bourne* and *James L. Mairs*

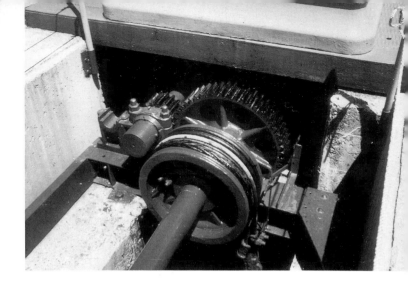

Machinery for opening and closing the locks remains as designed in the early twentieth century. Rigorously maintained, cables turn gears that engage teeth on lock gates. *James L. Mairs photos*

Along the waterway, hamlets and cities retain the canal-era look, with cupola-topped showplaces and recycled warehouses. *Above,* Middleport; *below,* Medina. *Russell Bourne photos*

Canal bridges must be lowered for crossing traffic; then, when an approaching boat blows its horn, raised back to the height of 15½ feet. *Russell Bourne photos*

This evocative photo from the 1940s shows three highways in New York's Mohawk Valley: the auto road, the railroad, and the enduring Erie Canal. *Erie Canal Museum*

Hauling the 60-foot barges loaded with 30 tons of freight put a terrible strain on the backs of the two tandem-yoked mules. To the end of their chain-and-wood whiffletree was attached a 250-foot-long rope, the towline; this line was secured to a post about a third of the way back from the bow on the starboard side of the barge. That system differed greatly from the traditional setup on an old riverboat, which generally had a truncated mast far forward; the towrope pulled from the top of that mast. The improved design of the Erie barges' tow rig balanced the forces more successfully and made it much easier for the helmsman to steer his craft away from the bank.

Captain and mule-driver were occasionally tempted to pick up the pace, wishing to reach the next town before night or to get the cargo to market sooner. But if the mules were whipped too hard, they would falter and collapse, so rigorous was the task of moving that weight and that 2 feet of draft through 3 or 4 feet of water. And despite the simultaneous temptation to overload the barges and gain more profit from a greater cargo, canny canallers recognized that that was counterproductive: the mules simply could not handle the task. It was not a matter of the added weight but of the additional water that needed to be shoved aside by the deeper-sunk hull within a restricted channel (a mathematical problem Ben Franklin had pondered in his day).

Drivers had little sympathy for the overworked mules, sorrow for their condition being expressed only when one of the valuable animals slipped and drowned—a frequent occurrence. Stories abound of cruel treatment. Revealing and painful "gallmarks" were often spotted by inspectors who (after years of driver malpractice in the first decades of the canal's existence) were sent out by reform-minded societies to examine the animals. While their two companions pulled, the two off-duty mules rode aboard in a cramped cabin built into the bow of the barge; entry to this "inside bridge" was made via a perilously steep ramp. To keep the mule from plunging down the ramp too fast, the driver would grasp its tail and hang on.

Mule-drivers, brutal to their animals and rough on their hoggees, brawled and fought their way up and down the canal. One captain confessed that he had employed a number of them who would "rather fight than eat." They were viewed as a happy-go-lucky lot, unencumbered by family ties. They were also known for drunken sprees after payday, at the end of each trip. Never did they seem to have enough money saved to get them through the winter. Instead they would repair to a canal town like Fonda where the jail had a decent reputation as an off-season haven. If a sociologist were to look at this category of canaller, he would probably conclude that while the mule-driver was not a slave to anyone, he was definitely not upward bound. Clinton's social modernization program left this person out—or rather made no provision for improving his lot, should he wish to have it improved.

Nor did the wretched hoggees benefit from any expansive aspects of the new society. Many of them were orphans, contemporary accounts inform us. Child labor was one of the ugliest aspects of nineteenth-century industrialization. And along with it went the cast off urban child—he begged, he hit the road, he possibly found a berth on a canalboat. By the middle of the century, a missionary estimated that there were some five thousand such barefoot lads and lasses on the canal, from all states of the union. Another gentleman of the cloth referred to the hoggees as "specimens of depravity."

Like the animal inspectors, the interfering missionaries were regarded as dreadful pests by canallers. A certain Deacon M. Eaton made a survey of canalside life in 1845 and tended to agree with the canallers that his colleagues were turning more people off Christianity than they were helping into it by their constant criticism of "the watermen" and their ways. One captain, while perfectly civil to Deacon Eaton when he came aboard, said, "As for praying, you can't [do that] on my boat."

Anthologist Lionel Wyld has spotted an important difference between the idyllic portrait of the barge boy in some ballads and the true picture of the hoggee as he appears in more authentic, less artistic verses of the day. In one of the ballads, the hoggee sings of his happy role:

> When I was young and about sixteen, none was more light and gay;
> I gamboled nimbly on the green or sported in the hay;
> The bloom of youth was on my cheeks, my heart was full of joy.
> But happy were those days to me, a merry boatman's boy!

But the mocking verses that the driver-boy often had hurled at him as he passed through a canalside village sounded harsher. One went like this:

> Hoggee on the towpath,
> Five cents a day
> Picking up horseballs
> To eat along the way!

Quite a contrast. And it's not difficult to guess which lines have more truth in them.

Life on Board

Barge-family children, considerably better off than hoggees, could be found in the cabins of the boats, along with father captain and mother cook. Canalside loungers could tell which of the passing freight barges (called "lineboats") had families aboard from the clothing hung out to dry above the cabin top. Barge-owning corporations generally favored hiring captains with wives and children, believing that family life "raised the moral tone." But the corporations did little to elevate the circumstances of living.

The cabin was usually in the stern, its floor two or three steps down from the aft deck. It measured something like 10 by 12 feet, with two built-in 36-inch-wide bunks at the forward end. A flimsy partition separated the master's "stateroom" from the living-eating section. Both this cabin and the stable forward were positioned above the main hold, into which freight was loaded through deck hatches; thus the heavily built wooden boats usually looked in profile like low-lying river barges, with only the two "houses" breaking the visual line of the gunwale.

In the cabin a coal stove glowed all hours of the day—even in the heat of summer. For relief from the heat, barge families often took their ease beneath an awning atop the cabin where the clothes were drying. It was reported to be a decent if difficult way to raise a family.

The chief difficulty was that so many children fell overboard and drowned. Another was that the babies kept arriving, with precious little room to house them as they grew. Extra sleeping space could be found on top of the hay in the mid-deck feed box; a child or two could bunk down there, free from family turmoils. It was by no means uncommon for a canalboat family to include six or seven children. We know something about how they all got along from vivid tales fortunately collected some years ago by the president of the American Canal Society and published in *Canal Boat Children*.

One fairly typical Erie canal mother had lost four of her children during their years on board: the oldest from "sunstroke," the second (five years old) by drowning; another by burning in an explosion; another (a baby) from spinal meningitis incurred when the child was accidentally dropped on the deck. On some boats the frequency of falling overboard was reduced by tying younger children to various objects on deck and cabin top. But when interviewed on the subject, a mother of seven children merely laughed and said, "Why yes, they are always falling in."

Just as soon as possible, the bargeman's children were expected to take part in the work. From the age of five on, both girls and boys assisted the mule-driver and even mule-drove themselves. Sometimes the child would ride one of the mules, more often walk beside it. A captain was quoted as saying that "the women and children are as good at it as the men." If it weren't for the children, he asserted, "the canal wouldn't run a day." And he admitted that his eleven-year-old daughter, who had been at the work "for several years," had been unable to attend school for half the school year. She was off canalling.

The wife of another bargeman was equally frank about the consequences of the lack of education: "The children are brought up on the boat and don't know nothin' else, and that's the only reason they take up boatin'. Boys work for their fathers until they're big enough to get a boat, and it's always easy to get a boat." The boy's dream was to become a captain by the time he was sixteen. Another dream was to earn enough money to buy a suit of clothes—an aspiration too high for a hoggee, who usually got the family's cast-offs.

During the season the days and nights of plodding up or down the canal continued without a pause. "It never rains, snows, or blows for a boatman, and a boatman knows no Sundays," explained one father. Another added: "We don't know it's Sunday till we see some folks along the way, dressed up and goin' to Sunday school." For those barge families that did decide to stop and tie up for the night, fifteen hours of work during daytime hours was usually expected.

Although barge families seem not to have suffered from lack of food, getting proper milk was frequently a problem. Mothers had to take what they could get from the grocery and feed stores that had established themselves at the locks and terminals. The more prudent families also obtained fresh water there, but many simply made do with the Erie's flow. Into it went all garbage, waste, and mule stall cleanings. From it came fish for the table, as well as turtle meat, served in stew and chowder. In it swam those children who had learned the art of swimming.

"Anything afloat always had my full attention," reported Richard Garrity, who in later years wrote of his childhood and growth along the "Upstate Waterways." Richard's grandparents had come from Ireland; his father and uncles had found jobs for themselves as youths on the Erie. One uncle had been killed at age fifteen by a kick from a horse or mule. His mother was from a German-descended family. At one point there were seven kids along with their parents in the Garritys' cabin house.

Richard survived a fall overboard when he was five. He remembered as one of the family's greatest tragedies the day when two mules drowned. He also remembered the fun of swimming and fishing, the joy of riding along and tossing a potato with a coin stuck in it to Italian immigrant farmers in exchange for some green vegetables they'd been able to bring forth from the black muck near Montezuma. Like his father, Richard adored the life and sought no other for all his days.

He and his family were aware of the contrast between themselves and the churchgoing, school-attending townspeople—another world. The mores and morals of the canallers seemed shocking to the townspeople. In their superstitions, their special language, their rude dress, the canallers were uninfluenced by contemporary fashion or philosophy, unmodernized by agricultural and industrial prosperity. Some of the canallers, to be sure, built themselves cabins at the edge of the town and tried to claim a share of the normal citizens' year during the winter, when ice shut down the canal. But many were content to stay aboard their boats then, as the boats sat upon the bed of the drained canal. Either way, they usually ended the off-season owing the grocer more than they'd paid him; the food for the next year's voyagings had to be obtained on credit.

There would be fights; the father of one of Richard's boyhood friends was knifed to death in one such fray. There would be fires, usually from the overheating of a cabin stove. There would be planning for the new year—the captains often owned two lineboats and had to be careful about coordinating the freight schedules. The winter dragged on and school was endured. But then came the exhilaration of the watering of the canal in early May. They were off down the towpath to Albany.

Lock Tenders, Toll Takers

Yelling "Hooraw—lock!" was the way Richard remembered he and his father would alert lock tenders that the barge was approaching. These men of the lock were a unique breed. Many had obtained their positions as favors from community judges and politicians. Most of them had an opportunistic side—they would favor captains who tipped them by locking them through swiftly—which put them in natural opposition to the bulk of the impoverished boaters. So, as remembered in myth, lock tenders tended to be mean and murderous and slightly "tetched," with a remarkable propensity for adulterous wives and comely daughters.

Exacerbating whatever personality problems the men of the lock may have had was the very real tension of their job. To be waked at all hours of the night by the captain's call, to unscramble a number of westbound line barges from a mess of eastbound log rafts, to be ever alert to the priority needs of the passenger-carrying packet boats . . . all that on top of the loneliness of many of the locations and the physical demands constituted an undoubtable strain. Lock tenders usually employed a hand or two to help heave on the heavy beams that swung the gates open—a design essentially unchanged since Leonardo's day. ("Tumble gates" were not installed until the next century.) The extra hands also caught the lines flung from the bargemen and became experts at the difficult job of snubbing those lines around a bollard so as to slow down the barge and stop it at exactly the right place in the lock.

Of course, not all the locks were in moody, isolated locations. The busily humming scene at Lockport, with its famous flight of five double locks, always appears in period photographs to be the very image of nineteenth-century vigor: mustachioed men in suspenders and bowler hats posed at their work stations. And at the other end of the canal—the side cut to the Hudson at Watervliet—the scene was equally populous. Here and at Waterford, where the lock tenders had a particularly low reputation, bargemen learned that a fight or a theft was as likely as a lift.

All tools and gear not "tacked down" would be stolen by these brigands.

To fuel the fights, there were twenty-nine saloons in the space of two blocks. The owner of one of the saloons, Paddy Ryan, won the title "King of the Erie Canal" for his victory over an English boxer in an eighty-six-round contest. Also known as "the Barbary Coast," for regularity of larceny and piracy, Watervliet afforded passing barges an average of one new body found in the canal each week.

Richard Garrity remembered that there were some friendly lock tenders who would assist a lineboat on its way. They would adeptly adjust the gates so an extra surge (or "swell") of water would start moving the barge out of the lock—thus easing the mules' task of pulling against an inert mass. But more often Richard and his family recalled the obstinate lock tenders who made them wait endlessly, favored traffic going the other way, exploited them by demanding tips or charging excessive prices at the store. Lock tenders who might be particularly vengeful because of a denied tip or a fight lost the preceding year also had a nasty trick of causing the lineboat to crash against the side of the lock, damaging it severely. With only about an inch clearance on either side of the hull in the Erie Canal's original locks, that "mistake" was easily perpetrated.

Lock tenders also came in for their form of picturesque abuse in the canal songs of the day. A favorite was "The Ballad of John Mueller and the Lock Tender's Daughter."

> John Mueller was a mule-driver
> On Erie's verdant shore,
> His walk was humble, but his gait
> Was something to adore.
>
> The lockman's lovely daughter
> Had for him a passion strong;
> Although she was both short and small,
> She vowed she'd love him long.
>
> Her father's haughty castle
> Stood beside the proud Mohawk;
> He did not lock her in the keep,
> But kept her in the lock.

And the story went on. Other stories told of jealous lock tenders who murdered their wives for affairs with canallers, of haunted lock houses, of fights and stabbings. It's difficult, even today, to see a picture of one of those stone or wood whitewashed lockman's houses (the "haughty castle" in the ballad above) and not imagine black happenings behind its deep-set windows. He was a limited man of great power, this lock tender, and the bargemen's resentment of that power seems to live on as a kind of curse.

For several decades there was another character on the canal with a reputation almost as unseemly as that of the lock tender: the toll collector. This was before the great day in 1881 when New York State, its inital loan paid back and revenues still flowing richly, decided to do away with the tolls. Early bargemen took every step possible to evade the tollhouses, attempting to sneak past under cover of night, even with the feet of their mules specially padded to quiet the noise. But eventually they resigned themselves to the inevitable reckoning with the hated toll collector. His ultimate disappearance was hailed, logically or not, as a great triumph for the bargemen.

In later decades there were other varieties of canallers who supplemented or assisted the activities of the bargemen. The state employed inspectors, for example, to patrol the canal and pay close attention to the condition of the banks—the berm was vulnerable to burrowing muskrats and eroding storms. These inspectors tended to be rather self-important and unloved. They riled bargemen with their constant insistence on lower speeds and no bank-destroying wakes. They riled townspeople too with their officious commands that no unauthorized travelers wander the banks and the canal right-of-way. Nonetheless, when a storm did threaten to tear apart the canal's wall, the entire community rallied to the inspector's call, rushing lanterns, wagons, sandbags to the jeopardized location. Samuel Hopkins Adams explained, "The Erie had brought a new and wonderful prosperity to [the people's] farms for which they were grateful. If Clinton's Ditch was in danger, they would put in their best licks to save it."

Whether seen from land or water, the canal hummed with life. This new animation of society was in itself a great change in the human condition—a change from those static centuries when serf had remained serf and slave had remained slave eternally. Here the whole watery world pulsated with activity, even at the lowest level of humanity. Walter Ed-

160

monds, rightly called "the laureate of the Erie Canal," referred to this stirring phenomenon as "the bowels of the nation . . . the whole shebang of life."

Before young Richard Garrity's fascinated eyes a delightful variety of boats passed up and down the waterway. "Bumboats" were perhaps the most looked-for, as they were the purveyors of household necessities and irresistible oddments. Though they often had their own means of propulsion, they gained their name from their masters' preferring to get a lift from some other craft. There were the boats of knife-sharpeners and dentist-barbers, tinkerers and entertainers, canallers all. Richard's own German grandfather, unable to forsake the Great Western at retirement age, bought an old barge, equipped it with a merry-go-round, and set out along the canal as a waterborne carnival.

But the question remains whether these several varieties of canallers—whatever the mood of their day, merry with carnival or angry with drunken rioting—were participants in Clinton's "modernization of New York society." And the answer appears to be negative; they were restricted by bonds of ignorance, and they could but infrequently advance themselves. They were unaffected by the booming wealth, the new industries, the Greek Revival celebrations about them; they raised no voice, cast no ballot in the formation of Van Buren's new political structures. They were stuck where they were. James McGregor Burns explains this status as a truism of the history of technology: the lowest class generally remains the victim of the existing technologies, its members being rarely "agents for change."

And that seems to be borne out to a certain extent by Richard Garrity's career: he stayed a canaller all of his life, watching the technology of the canal very slowly evolve around him. Along the Erie, despite the use of steam for such vessels as inspectors' boats, mules were used to pull the barges until just before World War I. That was the case even though the canal went through two major enlargements in the nineteenth century, one in 1835, the other in 1862.

With each enlargement, the size of the locks—and thus the allowable size of canal barges—expanded proportionately. The depth of the canal was also increased, allowing the passage of barges that drew 6½ feet by the time of the Civil War enlargement. To pull these massive barges, mules had to be double-teamed. But still the balance between man-mule on the one hand and nature on the other remained what it had been; life and the landscape were still looked at from the perspective of 2 miles an hour. Ultimately young Garrity roused himself and became a "fireman" on a steam-powered tug, and then an engineer, at 8 miles an hour. He would not leave the canal, but he had been partially modernized.

Packet Boats: The Fast Lane

From the beginning, the drama—and one might say the class—along the Great Western Canal belonged not to the freight-carrying lineboats but to the passenger-carrying packet boats. Brightly painted, with a slightly arched deck on which passengers could sit in good weather (if low bridges permitted), they were a handsome sight—as well as an economic boon. Indeed, during the first decades of the canal era, the packet boats were more numerous and more revenue-productive than the line barges. The word spread swiftly, on this continent and abroad, that the packet boats offered an exciting and inexpensive passage to the west. Hundreds of thousands of yearners for westward horizons bought tickets; each year nearly 100,000 westward-bound people were passing annually through the terminal in Buffalo at the height of canal operations, in 1845.

As early as 1825, a timely tour book for the Erie was published, produced by a G. M. Davidson of Saratoga Springs, New York. He advised would-be travelers of the "united considerations of . . . convenience, safety, and rapidity of this mode of conveyance." An awed trip-taker from Pennsylvania could scarcely believe the low cost from Albany, writing: "The captain actually engaged to take us to Utica, a distance of 89 miles, for one cent and a quarter a mile!! a York shilling for each meal extra, and to make no charge for births [sic], which are a very necessary accommodation as the boats run day and night."

For the bustling Yankee-Yorkers who were taking possession of this rich new world to the west, travel time from Albany to Buffalo was now reduced from twenty days on land to eight days on the canal. And the time was slightly less from west to east, though still restricted to the maximum 4-mile-an-hour rate. Posters and newspaper advertisements succeeded in giving the impression that packets provided a breathtakingly swift mode of traveling. Lafayette himself agreed. Referring to their passage along the completed section of the canal in 1824–25, Lafayette's secretary reported that they had "travelled rapidly and comfortably." If it was good enough for General Lafayette . . .

Somewhat later, another Frenchman named Michel Chevalier had even more to say about how much swifter and pleasanter was the Great Western Canal than its European contemporaries:

From our canals, which are navigated by heavy and clumsy boats slowly and painfully dragged forward . . . you can get no idea of this great channel, with its fleet of light, elegant, covered barks gliding along at a rapid rate, and drawn by a powerful team. Every minute boats are passing each other, and the boatman's horn warns the lock-master to be in readiness. Each moment the landscape varies; now you traverse large new towns, fine as capitals, with all their houses having pillared porticoes and looking externally like little palaces; it is an admirable spectacle of life and variety.

Every effort was made by the companies that owned and managed the packets and by their captains to persuade the travelers that this was, indeed, an admirable, valiant ship on which it was a great privilege to travel. Names such as *Rising Star* and *Cleopatra's Barge* graced the sterns. And the captain himself was the very model of a maritime officer, dressed and comported in the best traditions of service on the ocean waves.

The English novelist Captain Frederick Marryat (as quoted by Lionel Wyld) recalled his packet experience:

The captain of her was, in his own opinion, no small affair; he puffed and swelled until he looked larger than his boat. This personage, as soon as we were under-weigh, sat down in his narrow cabin, before a small table; sent for his writing-desk, which was about the size of a street organ, and, like himself, no small affair; ordered a bell to be rung in our ears to summon the passengers; and then, taking down the names of four or five people, received the enormous sum of ten dollars passage-money. He then locked his desk with a key large enough for a street-door, ordered his steward to remove it, and went on deck to walk just three feet and return. After all, there is nothing like being a captain.

Though courtly and commanding, these splendid characters could also be cruel and tyrannical to those beneath them. Skippers of slow-moving lineboats suffered particularly from the arrogance of the packet captains, both in confrontations at the locks and in the canal. Everyone had to clear the way for the speeding packet captain. The general system

163

for passing—for boats going either the same way or in different directions—was that one boat would swing out into the middle of the waterway and relax its towlines, letting the other boat surge past on the towpath side, its mules stepping over the loosened traces. Some captains were unwilling to wait for all that loosening to take place: sickles protruding from the packet's bow could be employed to cut the lineboat's towlines.

Captains employed by the packet companies lived in the thriving canalside cities, shared in the fast-paced life that increasingly characterized upstate New York, and occasionally entered into prohibited canalboat races, both for the purse and for the competetive fun of it. It was recognized that in the course of their regular routes on the canal, more than a few of them made fast-delivery reputations by breaking the speed limit, whipping hoggee and mules alike to the point where 6 or 7 miles an hour was achieved. If caught, the captain would slap down the $10 fine with great hauteur, knowing that his reward for beating the schedule would be far greater than the fine.

Fortunately for those who chose not to take such class-conscious, money-bent captains too seriously, a number of mocking ballads came forth. They mocked both the sanity and the tall-ship pretensions of these quarterdeck grandees. One verse of an oft-sung "comic song" entitled "The Raging Canal" went like this:

> The Captain came on deck and then began to rail,
> He hollered to the driver to take in more sail,
> The driver knocked a horse down and then gave a bawl,
> And we scudded under bare poles on that Raging Canal.

The competitiveness of the captains could best be seen in the city of Schenectady, where many passengers transferred to the packet for the cruise up the canal. Jostling other boats aside, ballyhooing the virtues of his craft, grabbing passengers right off coach and train and leading them forcibly on board, the brawny captain fought to fill up his cabins, then be off, hell for leather. "The Battleground" became the nickname for Schenectady among victimized passengers.

164

Floating West

They were in for quite a ride, those classy passengers. And suddenly, for anyone who wanted to observe the new breed of industrialized, modernized Americans, it was urgent to book passage aboard a Great Western packet. This included such transatlantic culture critics as Frances Trollope and Charles Dickens; the canal, as their readers knew, was the very definition of America at its most inventive and progressive. New and ever more vivid tales of the horrors and delights of the float trip across New York State were expected.

But the packets were not for snobs alone. Even as the literati were so preciously portraying the people and places of this New World, other less articulate travelers were streaming west on the Erie, all earthly goods wrapped in a kerchief.

The New Englanders who had been tempted to settle along this route for decades now speeded up their emigration, to the rate of ten or twenty thousand a year. In Rochester, the canal city with particular attraction for New Englanders, the population expanded from a mere thousand in 1817 to twenty thousand by 1838. A chronicler of the times wrote: "Thus the Erie Canal, as it became navigable . . . determined largely the type of people who should occupy our state." And as to their quality: ". . . the additions to the population are chiefly mechanics and artisans characterized by ingenuity, perseverance, and moral worth—which constitute the true riches of New England."

And besides the New Englanders, there were increasing numbers of emigrants from abroad—from Germany, from Ireland, from all parts of Europe where plague and revolution were squeezing the Old World. Those who could afford to rode on the packets; others had to put up with the lineboats (which made, at best, 50 miles a day as opposed to the packets' 80). The canal museum at Syracuse has made a laudable effort to track down and collect the letters and other revealing artifacts of these lower-class travelers. One woman's letter says much about them all:

My dear brother Liam—

My sainted husband Donal has died crossing the ocean. The good captain of this canal boat is writing for me. The children—thanks be to God—are safe but the three babies are down with diarrhea. Bless young Donal, sure he is quite a man now, just like his Da. I still have a bit of money left but that will soon be gone. I could take in laundry or find a family to work for in Rochester. I hope Donal's sister is still there. Ireland may be hard but without Donal it is worse here. I have never been so afraid.

Pray for your loving sister.

—Ruth O'Neill

165

Her letter, full of family concern and her own terror, is essential to keep in mind as other, prouder writings are paraded before us, full of upper-class drollery.

It was the low bridges under which the packet boats had to pass that caused discriminating riders (particularly those who enjoyed riding on the roof) to complain most loudly. The well-known song "Low Bridge, Everybody Down" is the garden-variety version of this complaint. Actress Fanny Kemble objected to the "humiliation" of having to prostrate herself on the deck whenever the cry went up that a bridge was coming. These "nuisances," as she called them, had actually been built by contractors to honor the state's commitment to farmers that cross-canal passageway would be provided to their fields lying on the other side; obviously the contractors had not bothered to build the bridges any higher than absolutely necessary.

A certain John Shaw who had come from England to take a "ramble" through North America complained bitterly that the "parties at the head of affairs [meaning in charge of the boat] neglected to apprise passengers of the danger" of the approaching bridges. Much as he grew to admire the United States as a "truly go-ahead country," he hated having his "brains knocked out by passing under bridges so low" that one could not appreciate sustained views of the countryside. He traveled, in fact, on a branch canal of the Erie, not on the Great Western itself; but his point would have been equally valid there.

Strenuous complaints were also heard about the sleeping accommodations—complaints heartfelt and witty enough to become famous as literature. The basic people-handling routine of the packet boat was that the narrow, cigar-smoke-filled cabin transformed itself into sleeping quarters at night; the forward part was the ladies' section, divided from the men's (on luxury craft) by a curtain. But let Charles Dickens tell the tale:

> Going below, I found suspended on either side of the cabin, three long tiers of hanging bookshelves, designed apparently for volumes of the small octavo size. Looking with great attention at these contrivances (wondering to find such literary preparations in such a place), I descried on each shelf a sort of microscopic sheet and blanket; then I began to dimly comprehend that the passengers were the library, and that they were to be arranged edgewise on these shelves, till morning.

The bunks were arranged so that three or four men might sleep one atop the other, and sleep or suffer through the night from the nearness of the neighbors in bunks above and below. But "bunks" might be too grand a word—they were nothing but wooden frames with canvas tacked to them. These were attached to the hull on one side and suspended from overhead on the other side by chains or ropes. When a rope broke or the canvas ripped, a special form of comedy ensued. A German traveler named Frederick Gerstaecker immortalized himself by writing the best account of how it felt to be a ripped-canvas victim:

I awoke with a dreadful feeling of suffocation; cold perspiration stood on my forehead and I could hardly draw any breath; there was a weight like lead on my stomach and chest. I attempted to cry out—in vain; I lay almost without consciousness. The weight remained immovable; above me was a noise like distant thunder. It was my companion of the upper story, who lay snoring over my head; and that the weight which pressed on my chest was caused by his body no longer remained a doubtful point. I endeavored to move the Colossus—impossible. I tried to push, to cry out—in vain. He lay like a rock on my chest and seemed to have no more feeling.

But when Gerstaecker finally resorted to the ultimate solution and jabbed his cravat pin into the interloper's backside, that individual instantly came alive, yelling "Help! Murder!" and leaping high enough for Gerstaecker to slide out from beneath him. Only then, in the dim light of the cabin, was the German able to see the ripped ruins of the bunk above and to understand what had happened.

No one seems to have complained about the food, however. It was tremendous—all three meals a day of it. A midday spread usually consisted of several kinds of meat, fowl, and fish, as well as potatoes, various breads, vegetables, and pickles and other condiments. For dessert there was a choice of pies and cakes. Since the packet-boat fare had originally been set at 4 cents a mile including meals, it did not take long for some Yankee-Yorkers to figure out the clever trick of coming aboard just at mealtime, stuffing themselves merrily, then departing with payment of a dime or so for the few miles traveled while dining. Howling-mad captains finally put an end to that.

Whether on packet boat or lineboat, the captain presented in ballads of the Erie is always yelling and screaming, like Lear or Ahab. Folklorist

Burl Ives delighted in characterizing a certain wild-eyed captain in his guitar-accompanied version of "The E-ri-e":

> We were forty miles from Albany,
> Forget it I never shall;
> What a terrible storm we had that night
> On the E–ri–e Canal.
>
> *Refrain:*
> Oh the E–ri–e was a-rising,
> And the gin was getting low,
> And I scarcely think we'll get a drink
> Till we get to Buffalo,
> Till we get to Buffalo.
>
> We were loaded down with barley,
> We were chuck up full of rye,
> And the captain, he looked down at me
> With his goddam wicked eye.

If you don't know the rest of the ballad as sung by Ives, you've been deprived.

But what those bunkroom and dining-room stories and all those songs that grew up around the captains and canallers really indicated was that here was a culture trying to laugh at, come to grips with, its own changed self. Individuals sang the songs and told the stories to communicate and explain the amazing group experience of riding on water across the land with all these wonderful characters. You might recall the journey as an adventure or (to repeat Fanny Kemble's word) a humiliation. But you came to see that all the personal elements—the passengers, the lineboat families, the lock tenders and hoggees—were in truth fellow players on an innovative stage. With them you were speaking a new language, finding your kind of fun, seeking your share of the promised harvest.

This was more than just another verse of the well-recognized epic of Americans surging West; it was the expression of a newly mobile, middle-class society. For the first time people-in-motion were recognized as what American life was about. These passing-through salesmen, these fortune hunters and evangelists, these factory owners' wives gone shopping, these perennial emigrants, were now seen as the mainstream of secular American life. The canal had created them, and they would go on in the future to make new worlds happen, by train, by plane, by interstate. Modernized indeed.

The New-Rich Yankee-Yorkers

Yes, it was the new people flooding into the canalside towns who made the difference. It was they who, in the phrase of Jesse Hawley, embodied "public prosperity" so remarkably. But they did not do it over-night—the opera houses, the academics, the Greek-porticoed banks. Nor did they do it, critics contend, with intellectually focused, broadly en-lightened social objectives. One of the affectionate but objective observers of early Rochester put it this way: "The means that have transformed the forest will not act upon the mind."

Let us go farther down-canal, to Syracuse, to meet the more fortunate category of citizens, those who unlike the canallers were modernized in a thoroughgoing, upwardly striving manner, confident of winning a larger share of the harvest. For Syracuse was the first community hit by the new wave of affluence—as well it should have been, for it was near here that the essential economic factor, the salt springs, were located. Yet its begin-nings were humble. "Do you call this a village?" journalist William Stone had asked a leading citizen in 1820. After surveying the swampy scene, Stone went on to answer his own question: "It would make an owl weep to fly over it."

The citizen whom he addressed, Joshua Forman (who, along with James Geddes, had been a leading activist in creating the canal), responded with total confidence. "Never mind. You will live to see it a city yet."

And but nine years later, with swamps drained, nearby lake reclaimed, and canal thriving, Stone was writing: "The county buildings are now being erected on an extensive scale." He added that within a generation the city of which he had recently made such sport would equal Albany. He recognized also that all that he gazed at in 1829—the "young ladies' school," the printing offices, and the vigorously sprouting law firms— were the creations of an extraordinary group of newly arrived zealots.

They had started with little but the potential of those salt springs at Salina. And these were both a problem and a boon, for the existing settlers at Salina were stuck in their old-fashioned ways; they were at first deeply suspicious of the big-talking newcomers next door. In those years at the commencement time of the canal—when the "chief productions" of the place were "salt, mud, and the ague"—the settlers' cabins were generally built of logs. The new structures for the canal workers, by contrast, were slab-sided. And many were the fights between the slabsiders and the log-cabiners.

But soon, as all citizens put themselves to the task and the traffic and the freight began to flow on the canal, Syracuse became known both for its production statistics and for the quality and urbanity of its canalside buildings—particularly the handsome, templelike weighlock (which still stands, serving as the Canal Museum). In 1825 a ratio of fifteen stores to four taverns had been achieved, along with Sunday rules and definite admonitions that boys could not run loose. By 1832 there were brick sidewalks and a population exceeding three thousand. Two years later, Syracuse counted four thousand citizens; the number of stores had risen to thirty-five, while a distillery and a brewery had been built to back up the dozen taverns.

After surviving a terrifying fire in 1834 and the financial panic of 1837, the city took stock of itself—and saw nothing but more boom ahead. "No improvement seemed too hazardous or difficult for these industrious folks," a writer of the day remarked. He may have been referring either to the well-executed city plan of Syracuse or to the industrial developments at Salina. At that once crude location, there was now a huge industrial campus: a plain of some 300 acres was covered with vats for the manufacturing of salt by solar evaporation. As a result of this activity, New York became the nation's leading salt supplier; by the time of the Civil War, nearly 60 percent of U.S. salt production was being shipped down the Erie Canal to eager markets across the land.

Attempting to enlighten the community were two good newspapers and three or four main-line Protestant churches plus a Roman Catholic church established in 1842. But the real heart of the city was the splendidly run Syracuse House. Its continuing prosperity and its welcome to new arrivals and passers-through gave the city its surging blood and vitality. To look at this hostelry more closely, however, is to see that for all the salt-rich entrepreneurs and land-boom millionaires who sauntered through its halls, for all its polite, information-dispensing managers and its handsomely dressed, efficient waiters, there was a strange monotony. Why did everyone appear so Yankee, so Anglo-American, so prosperous? Where were the emigrants?

They were in boardinghouses on the back streets, we learn from Theresa Bannan's *Pioneer Irish of Onondaga*. Even those foreign-born who might have afforded the fees at Syracuse House were turned away, such was the intolerance of the day and so determined were the successful strivers at the hotel to keep the Irish in their place. The wars that had raged in the early years of canal construction between the immigrant Irish laborers and the native-born Americans had now turned into a more polite but equally determined form of exclusion. If Syracuse, through its residential patterns and public buildings, was a revelation of the success of the social revolution in New York State, it was simultaneously a revelation of the limits of that revolution.

Young Lion of the West

While Syracuse shone as the star risen over the canal toward the east, Rochester glowed as a planet in the western skies. It was in Rochester that the dreams of the land speculators and mill owners turned into dazzling realities—though it could hardly be said, in cultural terms, that a golden age was here achieved.

Ever since 1823, when completion of the first section of the canal had allowed flour-mill owners to ship 10,000 barrels of their valuable product toward the coast, the city had prospered mightily. After the completion of its famous nine-arched canal-carrying aqueduct over the Genesee— recognized as the longest stone-arch bridge in the modern world—Rochester became even more effectively the center of the West's grain industry. No one disputed the rather grand nickname the city assumed: "Young Lion of the West."

The New Englanders, those swarming bees, were attracted to this center as if it were a garden of bee balm. They turned a rather crude, failed frontier town located upstream from Lake Ontario into a modernized metropolis astride the nation's main transportation corridor. Because of their postwar inpourings, the population rose from a mere 1,000 in 1817 and 1,502 in 1820 to 4,274 in 1825 (date of the canal's completion) and

11,000 in 1830. By 1838, the number had risen to 20,000, and the curve continued to sweep upward.

Although Nathaniel Rochester (responsible for the city's early name of "Rochesterville") and his land-investment partners had come from Baltimore, it was not those southerners who gave this town its character. It was all those mechanically minded tinkerers from New England. As well as getting their throbbing industries going, they were responsible for such organizations as the Mechanics' Literary Association (1835) and the Mechanics' Musical Association (1838)—founded "for intellectual purposes." But according to contemporary observers, there was something curiously leaden and pedestrian about these well-intentioned associations.

Whereas in 1816, after the devastations of the war, there were reported to be only two unmarried ladies in Rochester, the city was firmly in the grip of do-gooding wives and uplifting spinsters in the 1830s. One of the ladies' leaders was Sibra Ward Smith, whose family had come from Killingworth, Connecticut, and whose husband, Silas, having built the first store in Rochester in 1813, went on to prosper as a grain merchant. Three decades later, Sibra—who had founded a book club and had been active in the temperance movement, as well as in attracting such luminosities as Jenny Lind and Fanny Kemble to the city—was importing her dresses from Paris and London. She said that in the Rochester society she knew and loved, you could "fancy yourself in New York or else in Philadelphia."

But the house that she and Silas had designed and built in 1841 by architect Alfred Mason Badger shows all the dull ugliness of grandeur gone wrong. A block mass of ostentation, Badger's design for the Smith House stands in brutal contrast to the earlier (1835) elegance of the nearby Campbell-Whittlesey House. The latter structure appears to have been designed by that master of Greek Revival style Minard Lafever; it is endowed with all the interior grace and exterior balance of Greek Revival architecture at its best. Although the destiny of Benjamin Campbell, original owner of the house, was unhappy (he, a miller and merchant made rich by Erie Canal business, went bankrupt after only five years of residence), Rochester's Landmark Society has restored the house with period furniture as a reminder of the glories of the canal age. Glories not that evenly distributed, it would seem.

Like Syracuse, Rochester kept its Irish and blacks out of view, housing them in such squalid neighborhoods as Goat Hill. For the lower class, this was a tough city, its many injunctions against public drunkenness revealing how much of that behavior there was in the poorer sections. Charity there was too, but only along restricted lines: blacks were not accepted in the city's orphanages.

Another indication that all was not quite right with Rochester society at its richest was that it tended to be blue-nosed. Although a sparkling theater had been built in the city in 1840, it was soon shut down. A note in the Historical Society's archives explains merely that "popular opposition to the theatrical performance finally caused suspension." New York historian Carl Carmer levels consistent criticism at Rochester for its stodginess and for attempts to "buy culture" rather than to create or enjoy it; he finds the city "very much bound-up in mediocrity."

Carmer offers the intriguing explanation that the city was genetically too thoroughly Yankee-Yorker, having "not quite enough Germans to liven it up." Another explanation was given by an early settler from Connecticut, William Brewster. He wrote that the people among whom he then found himself were "plain men, plain and unaffected in their intercourse, style of living and manners. . . . No species of dandyism can exist in Rochester." The arts apparently represented to them the kind of dandyism that should be avoided.

During those early, disruptive years along the Erie, the announced end of the world caused great excitement in Rochester. Followers of William Miller had been informed that this Bible-based termination would take place on October 23, 1833; they should get ready. The summit of Cobb's Hill in Rochester was white with robed figures that day; farmers abandoned their harvests and came into town for the celestial event, climbing hills and scrambling up rooftops to be nearer heaven. There was really no doubt about the world's end—had the day not been preceded by a great meteor shower? But, strangely, nothing happened, and the Millerites had to revise their interpretations.

As the 1830s phased into the 1840s (and the nation endured one of its most damaging financial turmoils, the Panic of 1837), a new mood descended upon the citizens of Rochester. The creative enthusiasm that had buoyed them up during the 1830s—when they produced oddities

173

like an observatory shaped like a Chinese pagoda and mustered six-hundred volunteers for the war for Greek independence—was replaced by a far more conservative spirit.

No longer would be seen such wacky wonderments as buildings made of cobblestones taken from the bed of the Erie and local waterways [some sixty houses, schools, and stores built of these cobblestones may still be seen between Rochester and Niagara Falls]; no longer would there be the experimental octagons, the "hexastyle" Greek temples, the perfectly pro-portioned columned porticoes of modest public buildings. Instead, all would be grossly scaled displays of private ostentation or public power. Politically these people of western New York, who had once shaken up Albany with their ardent enthusiasm for the canal and for wider franchise now swung toward the reactionary, xenophobic policies of the Anti-Ma-sonic Party.

Talbot Hamlin, the insightful critic of the region's architecture, saw a relationship between the deterioration of style in the later years and the switch to more fundamental religious practices and more conservative politics. He wrote:

> It was no accident that [the 1830s] had been a period of strange sects [such as the Millerites], of free-thinkers, of all types of free-love communities that scandalized the righteous. The [conservative religious] "great revival" of the 'forties may have been partly a protest against the *aesthetic and moral freedom* of the 'thirties.

Hamlin also believed that the best period of New York's architectural creativity and religious activity occurred at a time when "the balance between a growing industrial system and an expanding agriculture was still held in some sort of equilibrium." When that equilibrium disap-peared—that is, when everything and everyone were industrially modern-ized—both the style and the courage deteriorated.

Free Love and Local Saints

174 Long before the 1830s–1840s transition, New York State witnessed the birth or arrival of a number of unorthodox utopian communities. First among them were the Shakers, who moved to New Lebanon (near the mouth of the canal) in 1787. Next, in 1789, the Community of the Universal Friend, led by Jemima Wilkinson, came to "Jerusalem," now

Penn Yan, near Seneca Lake. Both of these religious communities stressed celibacy and the communal life of work; though not attractive for long to new generations of adherents, they gave to New York State strong traditions of social idealism and slightly cracked religiosity. Both had more to do with their founders' imported beliefs than with the spirit of the land itself—the spirit that would so strongly influence later communities.

Blooming upon this land and from this society, New York's many new communities of the spirit were, to some degree, products of transplanted Yankeeism. In Carmer's words:

Prophets announced themselves and immediately disciples gathered about them. The movement of this idea frontier seems to have been from New England westward through the Mohawk Valley. This would account for the progress of Shakers, Mormons, Spiritualists, Oneida Perfectionists, and other advocates of unconventional practices.

But these American communities were also remarkable demonstrations of how in the midst of booming secularism and of social revolution, native religious themes assert themselves; the people find ancient gods for new times.

Of the several utopias that flowered along the canal in the first half of the nineteenth century, the most successful in its own strange way was that of John Humphrey Noyes. A real Yankee-Yorker and Yale-trained Congregationalist, he had been stripped of his preaching license because of his conviction that man's innate sinfulness had been redeemed through the Second Coming of Christ in 70 A.D. Then he was forced to leave his Vermont home as a result of neighborhood shock at adulterous goings-on within the communistic group that he had organized. Moving to Oneida, New York, in 1848 with his society of "Perfectionists," he attracted hundreds of converts to his hardworking, birth-control-practicing patriarchal community.

At the heart of Noyes's preaching about "social relations"—by which he meant sexual relations—was his belief that human jealousies could be done away with by the abandonment of private ownership, whether of a wife or of wealth. His people should be "Bible Communists," sharing all with each other and loving each other not in pairs but communally. Such an experimental Christian community, he trusted, would be tolerated in

175

the free air of New York State. Eventually, when the community prospered, Noyes went so far as to institute a system of eugenic breeding, called "Stirpiculture," by which selected couples (including himself and some of the younger women) were supposed to produce a new generation of particularly vigorous and intelligent young people. And so they did.

Noyes broadcast his theological news and his moral beliefs as they were revealed to him, and as the socioeconomic realities of his agricultural-turned-industrial community demanded. It all seemed to work extremely well—including the birth control (by "male continence"). Perhaps the wisest of the economic-survival decisions was that the community should support itself by making products which their salesmen could sell up and down the length of the canal, then nationwide: first steel animal traps and later silver plate. An attempt was made to equalize work between men and women; workers were paid on an enlightened wage scale. The industry prospered, modernization at its Christian best, it seemed.

But eventually Victorian moralists mounted an attack on this viable, radical social program that happened to coincide with a generational revolution from within. Noyes was forced to leave his many-roomed "Mansion House" and go into exile under cover of darkness. He left behind him not only a successful silver business (marketed under the name Oneida Community Plate) but also a canalside community with a unique heritage of sexual equality and patriarchal love. It was with something of a shock that residents and workers alike came to realize in the 1960s that those standards had slipped: executives of Oneida Limited were paid at just as high a rate, with just as great a gap between them and laborers, as obtained elsewhere in capitalistic America. Industrialization had been mollified here, not converted.

The fact that upper New York had been settled by people from New England areas where the mainline churches were not dominant did not mean that those denominations (Presbyterian, Anglican, Congregational) would not eventually follow along out the Mohawk Valley and to the West. They came in the form of missionaries on canalboats, preachers able to command audiences in both open-air meetings and imposing newly built churches. Increasingly conservative, they ultimately put the lid on the bumptious spirit of the region.

The outstanding leader of that conservative, revivalistic movement was the popular Presbyterian Charles Grandison Finney. This remarkably talented preacher—who had initially studied law under canal pioneer Benjamin Wright—took over his Rochester pulpit about 1830, when he was thirty-eight years of age. His manner of tracing with elegantly distended finger the downward course of a sinner's life was described by one captivated churchgoer: while that finger moved from ceiling to floor, "half his hearers [rose] unconsciously to their feet to see [the sinner] descend into the pit below."

Finney spoke often of the "strength of faith which I have been in the habit of seeing in New York." Others spoke of the region's "optimism, credulity, crudity, and superstition." He did not speak of the lack of equilibrium between modernized man and the natural world which would later trouble Talbot Hamlin; nor did he seek to find a reason for the popularity of his conservative message in the disturbing tumults of the canal era. Indeed, most writers see the explosive things that happened to American denominationalism here as merely outgrowths of a naturally spiritual region. Carl Carmer enjoyed referring to the "mystic quality of western New York State."

To understand the denominational frenzy along the canal and its national importance more completely, a comparison between Finney, New York's conservative evangelist, and Joseph Smith, New York's radical founder of the Church of Latter-Day Saints, may be helpful. Smith's *Book of Mormon* appeared in the bookshops of Palmyra, a typical canal town, in 1830, the very same year when Finney stepped up into his Rochester pulpit.

Joseph Smith's family was mentioned in Chapter 2, at the time of their leaving the scratchy hillsides of Vermont for New York's beckoning valleys. Joseph's father had had a history of failed schemes throughout New Hampshire and Vermont; he was now out in western New York, writing home that Palmyra offered great promise. So Lucy Smith engaged a neighbor to take her and nine children out along the Great Western Turnpike, making their way among hordes of other emigrating Yankees. For Lucy, the hope of establishing her family in a prosperous and cultured community was the dream that kept her going. Palmyra had already passed far beyond the rough frontier phase of the last century; nearby Canandaigua was known for its sophistication. Perhaps she could set up a little cake shop, find a place in Palmyra's polite society. But getting there was a grim struggle; by the time Lucy joined her husband, she had but 2 cents left in her purse.

Her youngest, Joseph, was exhausted. He had long suffered from a limp. But in the stimulating canalside environment of Palmyra he recovered his health, grew into a good-looking spinner of tales, and became fascinated by local stories about miraculous stones and native holy sites. He also agonized over the bitter denominational disputes among his mother's and father's new acquaintances. At age fourteen, he was so disturbed by these arguments that he begged God to give him guidance; two years later, on September 21, 1823, an angel named Moroni came to him and instructed him to start his own religion.

Carl Carmer urges readers to understand that the Joseph Smith story from here on—how he discovered the buried tablets, was martyred when in prison, and thus founded one of America's most astonishingly successful sects—is in truth a fascinating *folk* story. Others, including Alexander Campbell (founder of another authentic American sect, the Disciples of Christ), find in Smith's message only a melange of local New York superstitions and no great genius. Campbell wrote that the *Book of Mormon* contains "every error and almost every myth discussed in New York for the last ten years."

Whichever way his career is viewed, Joseph Smith drew from this contentious, modernized place and from his own inspirations a unique, enduring interpretation of the divine. The type of communality he preached seemed directly descended from the social message of New England's Pilgrim ancestors and from New York's early religious communities. His expectation that all laymen would participate in the priesthood of the church had a wide appeal. He believed in converting unbelievers by direct theological arguments rather than by overwhelming the emotions in the Finney manner. Those aspects of his leadership should not be overlooked by a later age which finds his imagery a bit quaint.

178

Charles Grandison Finney certainly did not have Joseph Smith's originality (or his court record—Smith had been caught in a slight indiscretion when young). It seems that Finney came from the gentler part of canalside society; he had earned a reputation as an accomplished horseman, marksman, and sailor during his lawyering years. An accomplished evangelist rather than an innovative prophet, Finney succeeded in touching the hearts of thousands.

Although it would be inaccurate to claim that the Erie Canal and its peculiar society were the prime focus of his message, Finney's tremendous revivals of 1826 and 1831 were deliberately programmed according to the rhythms of the canal. They took place in the winter, "before the navigation opens." Then, in the opinion of one of Finney's biographers, "commerce ebbed and ceased while an apathetic but penitent Yankee community contemplated its past and present sins." Or, as one of Finney's correspondents wrote to him, that was when people in the canal towns had "nothing to do . . . but to attend to preaching or pleasure."

Ultimately, however, Finney turned away from these rough, rich, and religious people of New York State's most mystical district. First he accepted the specially prepared pulpit of the Broadway Tabernacle in New York City, then the presidency of Oberlin College in Ohio.

All of these religious developments may, nonetheless, be viewed as distinctly canalside phenomena, related to those rich expansions, to that modernization, and to that lack of equilibrium. Though they all affected America's everlasting religious character, none of them could have occurred in any other place or time. All three of these New York leaders—Noyes and Finney and Joseph Smith—left the region, in exile, for martyrdom, or for further fame elsewhere. But what a remarkable indication of a perturbed society's capacity to generate new saints, new myths, new divine experiments and fundamental discoveries for the benefit of all.

At the same time, there was a generation of other sorts of folk figures here, not all of them so saintly.

The Rascal and the Infant

Near the western end of the canal, at Lockport, where so many laborers had struggled and died to execute the masterful design of the five double locks, speculators had a field day. With the constantly flowing water from Lake Erie, and with a fall of more than 50 feet from the upper level to the lower, these would-be developers planned to make fortunes from water-powered industries. But before such barons of the new age could get their cotton mills, their iron works, their aluminum factories organized, the land merchants had to have their day. If religious leaders could arise from or take advantage of these unbalanced times, so could scoundrels. It was in the guise of a land agent that a particularly wonderful rascal by the name of Colonel (of course) William M. Bond came on the Lockport stage.

The colonel, who arrived in town while the canal was still under construction, was a brother-in-law of Jesse Hawley, and thus was entitled to such privileges as a ride on the *Seneca Chief* with Governor Clinton to the Wedding of the Waters. Bond hailed from Keene, New Hampshire, and appeared to be a rather typical Yankee-Yorker (though gossips noted that he was divorced, and seemed somewhat disinclined to undertake serious work). His stated intent on arrival was to look after some land in Lockport that his brother had bought. But his true purpose was to grab a share of the golden harvest others were reaping here.

His first attempt was to buy land as inexpensively as possible from a gentle Quaker named Eseck Brown, one of the town's earliest investors. Mr. Brown had sought to protect himself from outside brigands by employing a local lawyer named John Comstock. Bond excitedly told Brown and Comstock that he was going to build a glass factory on the site he hoped to purchase at a bargain price, a modern factory that would attract a rush of associated industries and potential buyers to the remainder of the Quaker's property. Not totally taken in buy the colonel's story, Comstock insisted that Bond might have the property for a good price only if he would deliver on his promise to put at least $10,000 into this wonderful-sounding factory; it would have to be a first-class facility. Bond agreed, and the gentlemen shook hands, bowed, and walked their separate ways.

The problem was that Colonel Bond had nothing like $10,000 to spend on a factory. But as owner of a tavern named the Black Eagle, he had become acquainted with some canallers and other characters in town who might be helpful. He engaged one of these tricksters to run after Eseck Brown and ask him if he had not heard what terrible black smoke glass factories make, such dreadful outpourings of pitchy smoke that all surrounding properties would be rendered quite useless and unsalable. Well, the trick worked. Comstock was so aghast at the thought of his client's property becoming devalued that he demanded a meeting with Colonel Bond. The lawyer proposed that if no factory was built, Bond could have the acres under question for nothing.

After scoring this coup, the colonel felt optimistic enough about his future in Lockport to build himself the first brick house in town. It still stands, a grand and prideful example of how the revivalistic architecture of the day (in this case Roman Revival, strictly speaking, rather than Greek Revival) could by its very excellence pretend too much for its builders. Built in 1823–24 with bricks made on the site, it welcomes the visitor to its entrance hall as if to a splendid celebration attended by everyone. An elegant curved, self-supporting staircase (added slightly later) flows down from the second floor. At all corners of the squarish house are tall, well-lit rooms, each one a handsome space for the party to move into.

But all the parties that Bond had planned here—presumably for the other power brokers in town, among whom further deals could be made—came to a halt in 1831. The colonel had overextended himself; the state seized his holdings. He retreated to New Hampshire, where word was that he got married and involved himself with another canal, the Welland. There he ended his days, presumably with memories of that brick mansion, the dream beyond him.

At the other end of the social rainbow in Lockport lived men and women and children whose personal copings with modernization may have been less spectacular than the rise of Charles Grandison Finney or the fall of Colonel Bond but surely no less wrenching to the individuals involved—and no less indicative of the stresses within this society. There is, for example, the legend of a certain Mrs. Packwood who, babe in arms, was walking one day upon the high-arched canal bridge in the center of town. This was the bridge built over the chasm blasted out to let the waters flow evenly from Lake Erie to the Lockport level.

Like much construction associated with the early Erie Canal—indeed, like this whole canalside world—the bridge had been hastily, expeditiously built. It shook; there was no railing. The infant slipped from Mrs. Packwood's arms as she struggled for her own balance; horrified onlookers saw the baby plummet to the waters below and drown. In a fury at the canal that was supposed to have brought only wealth but had also brought disruption and tragedy, the citizens demanded that the bridge be torn town. The town fathers of Lockport complied, and the bridge was destroyed. But that was not quite the problem: men, women, and children were demonstrably no longer in balance with the world around them.

THE ALL–AMERICAN CANAL CRAZE

As NEW YORK CITY became the leading center of transcontinental shipping, storms of anxiety lashed rival port cities. New York's climb to prominence had begun in the first decade of the nineteenth century, when both proud Philadelphia and ambitious Boston lost increasing amounts of coastal tonnage to the convenient harbor on the Hudson. And when a stream of goods from booming new towns along the Erie was added to New York's total, there was indeed panic in other cities at the prospect of being eliminated as critical parts of the young nation's burgeoning transportation system.

In Boston, inheritors of the Middlesex Canal's limited destiny dreamed of linking their system with the far larger one to the west. The son of famous Loammi Baldwin (named Loammi as well) was selected as the most logical individual to investigate the thrilling possibility of constructing a Massachusetts-long canal which, having crossed the state, would penetrate the Berkshires and arrive at the Hudson Valley, ready to do business at the docks of Albany. Enthusiasm swelled as young Baldwin went about his survey. After all, if the Yorkers had been able to leap the Niagara escarpment without having known how they were going to do it when the project began, why should inventive Yankees not be able to

183

come up with some kind of tunnel or ramp or technological miracle to overcome their western hills?

That this question was given serious consideration—and that it was matched by other impossible-sounding canal schemes elsewhere—has tempted many observers to conclude that all Americans at this point had gone canal-crazy. They seemed to ignore reality and to regard the canal as an all-powerful tool, mightier than King Arthur's sword or even Moses's rod. By this tool, the impossible could be accomplished: the West won, fortunes for all, democracy reformed, power not to the federal government but to "the sovereign state." And when one considers what happened along the Potomac in Maryland, the crazy verdict seems justified. In order to take a canal across Maryland to the feet of the Appalachians, some $14 million was spent—an outlay which, as a proportion of the contemporary gross national product, was equivalent to putting a man on the moon 150 years later.

But in fact, Americans had not gone crazy; they had merely learned the wrong lessons from the success of the Erie Canal. They had learned that by throwing enough money in the direction of a canal project, a perfect and permanent transportation system could be brought forth and a national market for local goods stimulated along with it. They had not learned that to succeed in the construction of one of these frighteningly fragile systems, engineering genius and tight financial control were necessary. Also, proud of their own states' assets, they were disinclined to admit that the geological history of North America had somehow given an overwhelming advantage to New York State.

Nor had Americans learned from British experience the realities of excessive and impetuous investment in canals. In the uproarious 1790s, many a British fortune had been gambled away in a wild competition to equal the Duke of Bridgewater's success. Ignoring that and other negative evidence, Americans of means great and small prepared to sign up for shares in new and often impractical canal schemes and to participate in lotteries that were crooked from top to bottom. Canals were deemed geese capable of laying only golden eggs. What fool would not participate?

Nonetheless, a collective gasp was heard in the Massachusetts State House when Loammi Baldwin, Jr. presented the budget for his mountain-leaping canal. This presentation occurred only a year after the completion of the Erie, when all the world knew that New York's 363-mile-long canal (which had cost $8 million) was a solid success and believed that any state that wanted to duplicate the act should be able to do so easily. But when it appeared that the Massachusetts canal's cost would be nearly equal to that of the Erie even though the canal was not even half as long, the legislators balked. Baldwin's plan was defeated; apparently in this state, some *had* learned the right lessons from America's canal-building experience of past decades. Not many years later, the state backed a less expensive railroad venture that accomplished the same objective of reaching Albany; it did that by means of the masterful Hoosack Tunnel through the Berkshires.

In voting against a fantastic canal scheme, possibly realizing that Boston had no real hope of winning the race for control of shipping from the West, these prudent Yankees were out of step with the rest of the country. By contrast, the Pennsylvania state legislature, terrified that Pittsburgh was "doomed" as a commercial center because of the Erie's seizure of westward shipping, called together a special canal convention at Harrisburg. And in that very same year of 1826 (on July 4, of course), ground was broken for the construction of the "Main Line" canal that would, somehow or other, connect Pittsburgh with Philadelphia. The state-financed project was approved even though no one had a clue how to get over the Alleghenies. Certain optimists spoke of a tunnel—possibly 4 miles long—that would help the canal accomplish the impossible.

In fact, the tunnel never would be, never could be built. But the Pennsylvania Main Line Canal—despite its wild expense and weird technological solutions (a governor of the state spoke of its "prodigality and confusion)"—became the only system besides the Erie to overcome the Allegheny Front. Here were some people who had learned the wrong lessons, but had gone ahead more or less successfully anyway.

In this frantically competitive era of canal-building—roughly 1825 to 1845—there were generally three kinds of systems undertaken. The first of these, promised by De Witt Clinton himself, was a system of local links to the Erie (so that other parts of New York State would benefit) and improvement of that waterway so that lineboats of more than 30 tons could be conveyed along it. The second was a series of new canals in other regions (often not summit-level but lateral), some of them practical, others absurd. For example, Clinton was sufficiently flattered by the invitation to come and break ground for Ohio's two major canals that he temporarily quit work even in the deadline year of 1825 to rush out and wield a July 4 shovel in that midwestern state. Neither of Ohio's canals ever paid for itself; but neighboring Indiana's Wabash and Erie Canal was the most spectacular financial failure, burdening the state with $17 million of indebtedness.

The third type of canal built in this excessively optimistic era represented attempts to rival and outflank the Erie—most notably the Pennsylvania and Maryland systems. The canal from the James River to the Kanawha, considered as a possible route west by George Washington many decades earlier, might also be included. But this effort (which called upon the redoubtable engineering talents of Benjamin Wright and Charles Ellet, Jr.) never had a serious chance of succeeding; at one point the engineers dreamed of a *9-mile-long* tunnel through the Appalachians to complete the project.

Two awkward facts stand out as the era is reviewed: first, a crushing indebtedness was piled up by the northern states involved in these enterprises, totaling more than $60 million; second, much of the money was simply thrown away on technological fantasies, tunnels that could never be built, imaginary ramps that might have brushed the clouds. Considering this second point, and estimating that some two-thirds of the $188 million total of U.S. canal investment had been so wasted, Columbia University's Carter Goodrich recently concluded that canal-building was clearly a "mislocation of economic resources" for the nation at that time. Nonetheless, by the emplacement of these fragile canal networks that would be complemented (and then replaced) by railroads, the North established itself as a power of sufficient industrial and transportation might to win the subsequent war for Union.

Added all together, successful and disastrous canals covered more than 4,000 miles of the United States by the decade before the Civil War—double the total of industrialized Britain's canals. It was indeed a massive effort, perhaps wasteful but fundamental to the processes of nation-building and social change. Considering the number of frauds and scandals involved in building those canals and the victimization of immigrant workers, it must be added that this "social change," though it included the broadening of the franchise and the development of party structures, did not mean paradise was here attained. Yet according to one close observer, Alexis de Tocqueville, Americans by bridging their continent with canals "changed the whole order of nature to their advantage." They found their future by floating into it.

Augmenting the Erie

At first there seemed to be total enthusiasm for the new links to and augmentation of New York's Great Western Canal. Farmers of the Genesee River Valley and settlers along the Chenango (which would lead to the Susquehanna) joined timber merchants along the Black River in demanding that the state move ahead on promised construction of their waterways. Of all proposed links, the Black River—longest river completely within New York State, exiting into Lake Ontario near Watertown—was the route most technically daunting and least financially sensible. In addition, the project was the most plagued by corruption.

At first, the Black River project seemed to have certain things going for it. The river community of Long Falls had renamed itself Carthage, in the Yankee-Yorker manner, and was striving to become the region's mightiest paper-mill site; the marketing of timber products via canal would undoubtedly make for new prosperity and civility in this previously inaccessible and primitive part of the state. Furthermore, the greatest of America's canal engineers, Benjamin Wright, had surveyed the route and—even though he foresaw that there would have to be a total of 109 locks—pronounced the project feasible.

Authorized in 1837, the canal soon began to experience strange and damaging delays. Splendiferous hotels sprang up along the canal route, and industrialists made grand plans to use the canal water for driving the wheels of their mills, but no one seemed to devote much thought or care to the construction of the locks and other essential features. Rich contracts were given to builders who got the work done—slowly—and supplied the materials. Yet one had to admit that the local stone was not of high quality, and that the walls of the lock chambers seemed none too secure. Though at first local lads constituted the work force, by 1840 most of the workers were brawling Irishmen.

187

Finally, by 1850, much of the canal was functional, though the entire work was not completed, all the way to Carthage, until 1866. In its first year of use, some 25,000 tons of freight were carried up to the north country or south to Rome; by 1865, that annual tonnage had been tripled. But operation of the canal was casual or even sloppy, and breakdowns and maintenance problems developed. Pinch-penny tactics endangered the canal's integrity even as mill owners made fortunes.

Lock keepers and workmen tended to be hired on the basis not of talent but of party affiliation. One dam tender was so incompetent that he failed to open the gates during the heavy rains of 1869, with the result that the canal was washed out and the region disastrously flooded. By the end of the century, the situation had become so dangerous that the canal's inspector sent for Pinkerton detectives to investigate what was causing the scandalous number of breakdowns and breakthroughs. In the words of one regional historian, "The Black River Canal could never make its dreams come true as the Erie had a knack of doing."

On the Erie itself, the work to enlarge and modernize the canal was also carried out in a curiously lackadaisical way. Considering the fact that business was booming on the canal—with one lock near Schenectady reporting more than twenty-thousand boats locked through in the one year of 1833—it seems curious that the augmentation, approved in 1834, was so leisurely. Civil War pressures finally accelerated the work pace; in 1862, twenty-eight years after commencement, the new design was operational.

But, as on the Black River, fraud and profligacy characterized the work. A commission created to investigate the scandals reported, among other things, that there had been an outrageous "squandering of public funds in the construction of the [new] locks at Lockport through collusion of the Superintendent and contractors." It would be difficult not to conclude that the slowness of the work pace was directly related to the time required for mulcting more money from the project.

The basic program of the Erie Canal's redesign was to enlarge the channel and all allied structures so that heavier vessels could be brought into service. From its original dimensions of 40 feet wide at the surface, 28 feet wide at the bottom of the ditch, and 4 feet deep, the new channel would be expanded to 70 feet wide at the surface, 56 feet wide at the bottom, and 7 feet deep. That depth would allow barges carrying 240 tons—half a million pounds—to float along the Erie.

All locks along the route were to be "doubled" (as Lockport's had been from the very beginning), meaning that each would feature up-going water steps alongside down-going water steps. The locks' chambers were to be considerably enlarged, from 70 feet to 100 feet, big enough for barges of that length. Furthermore, efficiencies were to be achieved by straightening out certain curves and meanders; altogether, the canal would be shortened by more than a dozen miles. Although the total bill for the work was estimated at a colossal $30 million, healthy revenues and increasing traffic seemed to justify the expense. The tolls of one year alone (1842) totaled well over $2 million.

Nonetheless, irreconcilable opponents of the canal succeeded in arguing that state funds should not be squandered to improve the canal just because it was producing such a splendid revenue stream. Also, were there not technologically superior means of transportation that should be considered? Modern historians who have analyzed the motives of the anti-canal faction have concluded that key legislators were already under the control of the railroad interests. The fact that by that year 1842 (when a few railroads had begun to make money) only $10,000 worth of revenue had flowed in from that industry to the state seemed to confirm that a number of gentlemen were putting the welfare of the new industry above balanced investment policies.

In 1842, New York reactionaries succeeded in passing the notorious "Stop Law," which forbade any more work on canal improvement until a new state constitution was adopted in 1846. During those intervening years they intended to use canal profits to repay state debts, to build mostly unprofitable lateral canals, and even to make loans to railroads. It should be remembered that it was during this conservative era in New York State that the Millerites of Rochester turned out to greet the end of the world and other canal-area sects sought explanations for the rapidly changing world in radically fundamental dogma. The revolutionary excitement of the 1830s had pretty much fizzled out.

By 1842, work on the new locks at Lockport had been partially completed. (Although replaced by a different system in this century, these handsome nineteenth-century locks have been partially restored for view-

189

ers today.) And after 1847 the enlargement of the channel itself, which was the most onerous part of the project, inched ahead. At last in 1862, under wartime pressures, the new Erie Canal in its augmented form was open for business from one end to the other. By that time, revenues were totaling $5 million annually. But the conservatives and the railroad interests by then had done their work: in 1869, for the first time, freight hauled by railroads exceeded freight floated on canals.

It should be pointed out, however, that in the era before the Civil War, railroads were initially perceived as complementary to the canals. One of America's earliest railroads—the Lockport–Niagara Falls Strap Railway—serves as an example of this. Starting in 1836, it took tourists from the canal's most famous set of locks to the nation's most celebrated natural wonder. At first the little railroad cars were hauled by horses, a system which made the climb up and over the escarpment a continuing leisurely delight for visitors accustomed to the slow pace of the canal. After a few years that all changed, horses giving way to steam locomotives. The new age was at hand.

After the mid-nineteenth-century enlargements, by 1862, the Erie canal had a depth along its entire length of 7 feet; it could handle barges carrying 240 tons, quite an increase over the 30-ton capacity of original lineboats. And by 1882, the year when tolls were abolished and all boats could float free from Albany to Buffalo, the Erie Canal had earned $42 million beyond its original costs plus costs of enlargement, maintenance, and operation. Therefore, some ninety years after the beginning of Clinton's ditch, New Yorkers agreed with their leadership that another major transformation was in order.

Governor Theodore Roosevelt, following in the De Witt Clinton tradition, had proclaimed in 1903 that

the canals cannot be abandoned; . . . the present canal must be enlarged. We cannot afford to rest idle while our commerce is taken away from us, and we must act in the broadest and most liberal and the most energetic spirit if we wish to retain the State's commercial supremacy.

His audience of believers listened and obeyed, approving a larger bond issue than ever before approved by any state—$101 million. Fifteen years later a new generation of trained engineers and unionized construction workers completed the New York State Barge Canal, financed (as of old) by the state itself. With locks more than 300 feet long and 43½ feet wide, it can accommodate barges carrying as much as 3,000 tons of cargo. And because it embraces the Champlain, Oswego, Cayuga, and Seneca canals as well, the Barge Canal (which, despite its name, is now used primarily by pleasure boats, more than 100,000 of them a year) also carries out Clinton's promise. It shares the benefits of the central canal with the outlying parts of the state, and with the nation as a whole.

Opening the Interior

From the first rumors of its success, the Erie Canal and its branches stimulated dreams of facilitated agricultural transportation and invigorated water-powered industry in other regions. In New Haven, Connecticut, former home of many Yankee-Yorker émigrés, envious citizens read letters from westward-traveling relatives about floating along the stretch of the Erie opened between utica and Rome in 1819. By 1822 the stay-at-home Yankees had organized themselves; they determined to recapitulate the miracle of the Great Western. A January meeting in Farmington of representatives from fourteen affected towns concluded that America's best engineer, Benjamin Wright, should be retained to build a canal that would run 86 miles cross-country from New Haven to Northampton, Massachusetts, a port on the middle stretch of the Connecticut River.

In this way, Connecticut sought to take part in America's canal revolution. What particularly pleased the planners in New Haven was that this canal—subsequently called the Farmington Canal—would completely outflank Hartford. It would, in effect, make New Haven the mouth and major port of the mighty Connecticut River. Protesting Hartford merchants could go hang.

Wright presented his positive report in April 1822, and by May 30 a state charter had been granted to construct the waterway. Things moved swiftly at first, despite the difficulties of the engineering challenge: in order to take the canal 292 feet to the summit (at Westfield, Massachusetts) and 213 feet down to river level, some sixty locks were called for, twenty-eight of them in Connecticut. An aqueduct of heroic proportions was needed to carry the canal across the Farmington River; banks leaked;

191

a kind of floating bridge had to be invented to take the canal path across intervening ponds; the hydraulics of feeders and sluices had to be worked out as if for the first time. Nonetheless, the first section of the canal, from New Haven to Farmington, opened with great fanfare in 1828.

For such a little state, Connecticut's celebration might seem a bit vainglorious: no less a figure than contemporary America's greatest historian, George Bancroft, hailed the marriage of the waters of Long Island Sound with those of the upper Connecticut. And subsequent difficulties along the waterway—lack of profits because of cost of repairs, reports of excessive cruelty to both mules and hoggees along the towpath, and failure of any towns but New Haven to come through with extra needed capital—raised the question of whether the canal had been a good idea in the first place. But for the nineteen years of its operation (before the New York, New Haven & Hartford Railroad claimed and clobbered it), the canal succeeded in tremendously stimulating the region's agricultural economy, in completing the dream of tapping New England's interior, and in giving many a villager such a pleasant ride across the countryside that his descendants still envy him.

It was neither passengers nor agricultural goods, however, that impelled the remarkable network of lateral and summit-level canals in mid-Atlantic New Jersey and Pennsylvania. Here the objective was simply to get the anthracite coal out of the tight folds of the Appalachians and into eastern ports. (Later the transport of iron and steel also played a part in the canals of this vital region.) Although the initial link in this system was the Schuylkill Navigation Canal (dreamed of by eighteenth-century Philadelphians, but actually built at the same time as the Erie, 1815–1825), that was soon overshadowed by the ambitious Lehigh Canal, 1818–1829.

Despite sharing its era of construction with the modernizing Erie, the Lehigh continued to reflect the mind-set of eighteenth-century Federalists. It was the private property of two collaborative speculators, a dreaming Quaker named Josiah White and a technically skillful former New Englander, Erskine Hazard. Their development of the Lehigh River, under the name Lehigh Coal and Navigation Company, made them the first industrialists to own a major American river. But a more important distinction was that in their great ambition to facilitate and control the shipping of coal from these mountains to the sea, they executed a design of astonishing magnitude with admirable gumption.

Having obtained their charter from the state of Pennsylvania, the partners set about the business of building their 65-mile canal across the land's rugged face. Lack of experience seemed no impediment; they worked in the swirling waters of the riverbed along with their laborers, demanding and giving only the best. White even created a different design for the numerous locks. These "bear-trap" locks—in which the gates blocking the river's waterflow are raised upward from the chamber floor by flotation rather than swung in from the sides by human muscle power—are still being discovered along the route as ancient ruins, testaments to local genius.

But the most amazing aspect of the design was that the partners insisted that all elements of the waterway be big enough to bring *ships* up from Easton on the Delaware River to the terminus at Mauch Chunk. Yes, ships, in the manner of France's Canal du Midi. For that reason the lock chambers were immense, measuring 30 feet wide by 130 feet long (later cut down to 22 by 100 feet). This contrasted strikingly with the dimensions of the subsequent, state-built Delaware Division Canal, which was to carry the coal barges down to Philadelphia; that channel was no more than 11 feet wide.

Furthermore, though White and Erskine had been able to overcome a host of technical problems and get their hillside canal completed with a minimal work force, it appeared as if the state would never finish the easy-gradient Delaware Canal no matter how many men or dollars were flung at it. Finally the state had to bow to the inevitable and request the partners to take over the project. It was a complete reversal of the situation in New York, where the state had proved itself the omnipotent force, rising triumphant above local interests.

There were to be many other surprises in this mid-Atlantic theater of canal-building as zealous individuals and officials raced to take advantage of the new technology. Foremost among these projects was New Jersey's famous and successful Morris Canal, built between 1824 and 1831—the world's most elegant inclined-plane system. The New Jersey canal-builders (whose objective was to get Pennsylvania coal up and over their state's highlands to waterways leading to New York Harbor) faced the awesome challenge of surmounting a summit far higher than that of the Erie: Lake Hopatcong, the Morris Canal's summit, lay 914 feet above tidewater. At first survey, it appeared that some two hundred locks would be necessary to get the boats over a total rise-fall of 1,674 feet, along a meandering route of 102 miles from Phillipsburg, New Jersey, to Newark. But the dreamers made their fantasy come true, in a unique way.

Here it was not Yankee cleverness that won the cause; it was British experience. James Renwick, the noted English engineer, was retained to provide the expertise. He judged the height too great to be conquered by locks alone—this was, indeed, the greatest height to be attained by any watered U.S. canal—so he created a spectacular design combining twenty-three inclined planes and twenty-four locks. The planes were actually a double series of marine railways, with up-going boat cradles balanced against down-going boat cradles. A massive hemp hawser turned by an ingenious underground water turbine (fed by water from near the summit level) gave the cradles an extra lift.

Another ingenious feature of the Morris Canal was that both cradles and boats were built in two sections, connected by a hinge; this allowed the entire carriage and cargo to bend over the "hump" at the top of the plane, facilitating upward movement and entrance into the lock of the waterway above. The planes varied in steepness from one-in-ten to one-in-twelve; the longest, at Boontown, had a rise of 80 feet, much more than a lock of the day could have accomplished. By Renwick's combined system, coal barges weighing 25 tons (later, when the system was enlarged, 100 tons) were successfully hauled-floated east for many decades after completion in 1831. Despite competition from the railroads, barges kept moving up and down the planes of the Morris Canal until 1924.

Indeed, here again Americans of the day saw a complementary relationship between railroads and canals—though many historians still insist that the former wiped out the latter with massive inevitability. In fact, considering only the coal-carrying canals, it was much cheaper, ton for ton, to ship by canalboat than by railroad car. Studies by William Shank, president of the American Canal Society, demonstrate that several railroad companies of the mid-nineteenth century "acquired canal lines and kept them in operation as long as canal maintenance did not become a problem." Canals, having led the way, continued in a humble manner to assist the boom-and-bust American economy.

In this process, the design and carrying capacity of the canalboats improved but little. To be sure, planners of the Morris Canal (and, later, Pennsylvania's Main Line) found inventive ways to shape and bend their boats so as to improve efficiency. But generally, the history of canalboat design is more static than inventive. The old barges seemed to work well enough at their slow-paced, brutal, bottom-of-the-economy job, so why improve them?

In the post-Revolutionary decades, 60-foot "Durham boats"—heavily but shallowly built to float 15 tons of Robert D. Durham's iron down the shoals of the Delaware River—had been adapted for use on the Schuylkill Canal. Expanded to 100 feet, but retaining the 2-foot draft, these became the grandfathers of canalboats everywhere, replacing the even more ancient river "arks" or rafts. Lineboats, with their sturdy, oaken, blunt-bowed forms, appeared to have joined the list of unchangeable American maritime shapes, along with canoes and whaleships. Only when the Erie was deepened and steam replaced mule did today's steel and concrete hulls begin to evolve, with more elaborate steering gears and complex devices for yoking pairs together. Brilliant examples of naval architecture canal barges neither were nor would ever be.

Wonders of the Main Line

The innovative spirit of the canal-building era reached a kind of wild epitome in the system banged together by Pennsylvanians to rival the Erie. This system had its origins in the panic that seized Philadelphian breasts when consequences of the completion of the New Yorkers' canal were fully understood. Beyond the fear that Pittsburgh was "doomed," terror piled upon terror. Putting this panic into historical context, one writer explained:

From the yellow fever epidemic of 1793 to the demise of the Bank of the United States [located in Philadelphia] in 1841, Philadelphia suffered a series of urban traumas that undermined its corporate confidence and its citizens' wealth. One of these traumas was the opening of the Erie Canal, which snatched away from the city its dominance of western trade.

Yet the pathfinder to the city's economic salvation was immediately at hand, a brilliant civil engineer named William Strickland. He was sent to Europe by the hastily organized Pennsylvania Society for the Promotion of Internal Improvements, commissioned to figure out the best transportation solution for the state. And in England in 1825, he first gazed on George Stephenson's famous railroad-car-pulling locomotive, the *Rocket*. Soon thereafter, Strickland wrote, in a report that deserves greater recognition for its imagination and sanity, that when it came to a consideration of transportation systems, "railways will receive a preference."

By no means did Strickland regard canals as inferior or obsolete or to be canceled. His report embraced "Canals, Railways, Roads, and Other Subjects"; he remained an impartial observer with an understanding of the virtues of each. Yet by alerting other minds to the steam-powered technologies of the future, he would help give Pennsylvania its locomotive-building industries and its railroad-based destiny.

Many Pennsylvanians were so excited by the image of canalboats floating over the mountains (and so captivated by the sound of canalboat tolls falling into New York state's coffers) that they could not credit what Strickland had to say. They believed only in the eternal superiority of canals. And, calling together the Harrisburg Canal Convention of 1826, they succeeded in shaping affairs so that the first shovelful of soil for the Main Line Canal was turned by the governor in the state capital on July 4 of that year. No one worried excessively about precisely where or how the canal was to go; instead, Pennsylvanians buoyed their enthusiasm by calling their imagined system the "Grand Canal."

Two years later, the final course of the route had been sketched out, though there was still no definite plan for how to get over or though the Alleghenies. And one year after that, in 1829, the state was in a financial pickle; $1,398,000 worth of debts had been accumulated and $2,060,742 worth of builder contracts had been signed, with many more still to come. The canal commission, which had borrowed $8,260,000 from state banks, could see that an enormous deficit was in the making—in fact, Pennsylvania's initial program was going to cost the state a colossal $15,500,000 (as against New York State's $10,946,352 for the Erie's cost plus interest). By the 1830s, interest on Pennsylvania's canal-caused indebtedness rose to $1,870,000 a year. Compounding the problem, scandals in connection with lotteries to assist the canal had become so notorious that that form of extra funding was finally banned.

A scheme of raising construction money by increasing taxes on farmers along the canal route (on the theory that their land values would be increased) succeeded only in alienating the citizens who had at first been solidly behind the project. But some such tax had to be put into effect, since Pennsylvania had no prime product like New York's salt on which sales fees could be levied and income projected. Furthermore, the costs of shipping from west to east, though lowered, were still so high after completion of the canal in 1834 that farmers continued to send their produce to the coastal markets via New Orleans. Only a decade after the canal's completion, it was clear to state policy makers that they had better get out of the canal business, and sell to private interests.

But the financial high jinks along the Main Line or Grand Canal were nothing compared with the gymnastics of the system itself. By the time it was completed, canal travelers progressing from Philadelphia to Pittsburgh had to make no fewer than thirty-three changes of power mode—that is, from mule to steam to horse to cable. The whole 395-mile system was a cobbled-together linkage of lesser systems zigging and zagging through the tightly folded mountain valleys and crucial water gaps of the state. The whole was never more than the sum of its parts.

One of Pennsylvania's more successful early canals was the Union, completed at about the same time as the Erie. Connecting the Schuylkill and Susquehanna rivers, it ran from Philadelphia northwest to Reading, then southwest to Columbia. Along with its ninety-three well-built locks, the Union had other virtues (and a few quirks, such as the steam-driven pumps that raised water to summit level). So, originally, the cross-state canal-dreamers thought that this twisty route would make an acceptable first link. But more sober heads pointed out that the Union was too narrow for the kind of Erie-rivaling traffic that was anticipated.

To offer an attractive alternative, a new waterway 40 feet wide at the surface and 28 feet wide at the bottom of the channel was planned; locks would be 90 feet long and 15 feet wide. But then, abandoning this plan and the Union (which continued to function profitably as a coal-carrying canal until 1901), the Main Line's builders projected a straight railway line between Philadelphia and Columbia on the Susquehanna River. That rail link, with horses pulling railroad-wheeled coaches along iron tracks, would start travelers west on the Grand Canal to Columbia, on the Susquehanna.

197

Arriving in Columbia, the travelers were then expected to climb aboard boats for a true boat ride. This waterway link, roughly paralleling the Susquehanna and Juniata rivers, took them 173 miles farther west and, thanks to 111 locks, conveyed them upward to a boat basin at the quaint town of Hollidaysburg, elevation 910 feet. Here the "Eastern Division" of the Main Line Canal (completed in 1832) abruptly stopped, all passengers off. For Hollidaysburg was situated at the base of Allegheny Mountain—a barrier that towered 1,398 feet above the town. Early arrivals here had no choice but to catch a ride on one of the awkward wagons that lumbered up and over the mountain on the rutted, washed-out Cambria Turnpike.

The same obstacle faced travelers approaching the mountain from the west. The Western Division, started at the same time as the Eastern and built by squads of Irish recruits, proved somewhat easier to complete. The route entered the Allegheny fastness by means of the tempestuous Conemaugh (meaning "beaver") and Little Conemaugh rivers; canalboats were to be lifted by sixty-six locks, landing in the basin at Johnstown, Pennsylvania, elevation 1,154 feet. By 1829 much of the Western Division was completed—not including a massive aqueduct that had to be built at the Pittsburgh terminal (where the Main Line joined the Ohio River, leading to the glories of the West). But the impossible, mountainous 36 miles between Johnstown and Hollidaysburg still blocked the way.

The decision about how to beat the mountain was finally made in 1831. Rather than push ahead with the technically unfeasible plan of boring or blasting a 4-mile tunnel through the summit, and rather than build a spiraling railway up and around it (the gradient would have been too steep), the legislature approved a plan to overcome it by inclined planes. This would not be a matter of planes alternating with water passages as on the Morris; these would be planes and levels all the way: five planes up the steep east face to the 2,291-foot summit and five planes down the more gradual western face. The question was what would supply the lifting power?

Engines for Change

Although the "levels" between the top of one plane and the bottom of the next were considered flat enough for carriages to be pulled along tracks by horses (later replaced by locomotives), fixed steam engines were deemed to be the only force mighty enough to haul carriages up the planes. Some of the planes were as steep as 9.9 percent (that is, a 9.9-foot rise along a 100-foot distance), lifting the carriage 200 or 300 feet skyward. To haul loads of 7,000 pounds up against that resistance, massive 35-horsepower stationary engines were installed—twin engines, in fact, one for a work-horse, one for a spare—in engine houses at the head of each plane. The size of the cast-iron equipment can be imagined by reading an inspection report from 1833: the inspector found that the larger engines had boilers 20 feet long; cylinders powered by the boilers' steam were 14 inches in diameter, driving pistons a stroke distance of 5 feet.

The pistons activated a crank that turned a wheel taller than a man. Around this "sheave" was wrapped the continuous hawser that pulled the carriages up. From that vertically positioned sheave, the hawser went down into the basement and around a horizontally positioned sheave before coming up again, around another vertical sheave, and thence down on rollers between the ramp's rails to the bottom of the plane. All of the huffing and whirring engine-house machinery was in a pit below the floor, leaving the way clear for a carriage to pass through the house without obstruction—the delicate business of connecting and disconnecting the lines being undertaken by a well-trained crew of "hitchers." The weight of down-going carriages assisted the engines in the task of hauling up the ascending carriages.

For years after the opening in 1834, this dangerous experimental contraption worked amazingly well. It was known far and wide as the Allegheny Portage Railroad—which today remains the name of the national historic site that recreates key segments of the railroad. And the effort seems worth making, for this is indeed an astounding, however primitive, piece of American engineering.

During the Portage Railroad's busiest years, six cars were being pulled up the inclines every hour, and some thirty-five boats went through Johnstown each day full of passengers headed west. Contemporary accounts indicate that traffic was so heavy day or night that one could see at least forty boats (most of them carrying westbound freight or passengers) at any gathering place along the canal. Most remarkably, passenger travel time from Philadelphia to Pittsburgh was reduced from twenty-three to four days (1840). Although the operation at each engine house must have looked and sounded wild and terrifying, the whole thing worked brilliantly.

Of course, there were ghastly accidents—exploding boilers, broken hawsers, runaway cars, crushed bodies, and crunched fingers. But generally the Portage Railroad performed well enough to be hailed as a unique triumph, another indication that American had entered fully into the industrial revolution. Easterners and foreigners hastened to come see the western miracle for themselves.

To protect the increasing traffic from additional disasters, safety devices were improved. The danger of a loose and slipping hawser was prevented by means of a weight rigged to keep the horizontal sheave in proper tension; the hemp hawsers (which measured more than 11 miles altogether and had originally cost $20,531.05) were eventually replaced by wire cables. Another on-site invention was a spring-loaded friction brake car or "buck," which rode ahead of descending carriages, looking something like a cowcatcher. Its purpose at times of cable breakage was to prevent cars from charging downhill to destruction.

And despite the engine houses' ramshackle look (which a kindly architect might call "vernacular"), much of the Allegheny Portage Railroad's construction was carried out with excellence. A lead example of this is the Skew Arch Bridge (1832), a majestic and still-standing masonry span which enabled the preexisting Cambria Turnpike to pass over the railroad near the top of Plane Six. The engineering problem here was that the intersection was not at a right angle. Thus the abutments for the turnpike's bridge could only be set up diagonally across from each other, and the stones for the arch all had to be cut on the bias. The results—particularly as the rising sun shines through the arch on a crisp morning—are extraordinarily handsome.

Also effective if eccentric was the innovative design worked out for canalboats on the Grand Canal, a design forced into being by the peculiarities of the Portage Railroad. The story of this development begins with the arrival of a certain Jesse Christman with wife and family on their own boat at the Hollidaysburg basin in 1834. The boat's name was *Hit or Miss*—nicely evocative of the spirit of the day and of the mood in which this young family had undertaken their westward migration, accompanied by household goods and livestock. Jesse's intention was to sell his boat at the basin and to go the rest of the way to Pittsburgh by the usual combination of railroad cars and canalboats. But in talking his way around the waterfront he encountered an imaginative fellow who seemed to have a better idea.

This was John Dougherty, an enterprising Irishman known variously to friends and enemies as "Forwarding John" and "Agitator Dougherty." Dougherty's on-the-spot idea was that Jesse's boat could be loaded upon a flatbed for one of the carriages, carried up and over the mountain with all its contents aboard, and deposited into the canal at Johnstown, ready to continue the voyage. The Christmans, who thought this sounded like a great adventure, soon found themselves being carried up the mountainside. By nightfall their boat had sailed to the summit (many travelers stopped there for the night, though the entire trip on the Portage Railroad required only six hours). And the next morning, having made the descent, they found themselves cruising westward toward the Mississippi Valley, where they would make their new home.

Although John Dougherty's own shipping business ultimately failed, his forceful creation of a new boat-carriage system—based on the Christmans' experience—put him briefly in a commanding role. His design called for canalboats to be built in three or four joined sections; each watertight section could be separated from its colleagues upon arrival in the basin, then set upon a flatbed and easily carried over the mountain. Pushing his idea before the consideration of the canal commissioners, Dougherty eventually saw the concept fulfilled: most of the boats that left from Philadelphia's Broad Street in the latter 1830s were of this sectional design, prepared to keep all passengers and goods aboard as they made the journey from Hollidaysburg to Johnstown. This made for a far more efficient system, something like today's practice of containerization, even though the Grand Canal still had far too many wrinkles to be regarded as smooth and simple.

A Dollar a Day, Canallers' Pay

On the countryside through which it passed, the social changes brought about by Pennsylvania's stapled-together railroad-canal were extraordinary. In the words of historian John F. Coleman:

The coming of the Allegheny Portage Railroad altered the conditions of life in Cambria County in a host of ways. It quite literally thrust a heretofore isolated, rural and provincial people into the mainstream of nineteenth century American life. The county suddenly possessed what was in that day a swift and reliable system of communication with the great cities to the east and west, with the Atlantic Ocean and the Ohio Valley. Through its fields and valleys passed an ever-swelling stream of goods, and across its borders came a fascinating procession of new faces: boatsmen, businessmen, migrants, wagoners—and poets, presidents, and statesmen.

The growth rate of Cambria County from 1830 to 1850 was, at 250 percent, exactly double that of the state at large.

At one end of the social spectrum there were the aggressive entrepreneurs, men like John Dougherty who had bursts of prosperity and, occasionally, crashes to failure. At the other end there were the canallers and workmen who made the hardware along the Portage Railroad click and spin. Or, to look at the social situation vertically, at the top (literally at the top of Allegheny Mountain) there was the solid stone inn built by Samuel Lemon, who succeeded in making himself one of Pennsylvania's richest citizens as a result of his hustle along the Portage Railroad; down the hill from Lemon House, by way of contrast, was the Blair County Poorhouse, whose numbers of indigent and helpless immigrants swelled as the 1830s rolled through the 1840s to 1850, when it contained several complete, permanently installed families.

On boats along the water stretches of the Main Line Canal, bargemen's wages were in keeping with low standards elsewhere: $60 a month for the captain, $25 for steersman, and $5 to $10 for mule-driver, depending on age and experience. Landside workers seemed to fare somewhat better, with most getting a solid $1 a day but some (including carpenters, blacksmiths, and engineers) making half again that amount. Curiously, the fellows at greatest risk—the hitchers, firemen, and switch tenders—seemed to make the least, only 87½ cents a day.

What made the workers' lot even worse was that they were paid irregularly, with gaps that often stretched to three and four months. Forced to obtain credit from local businessmen, they increasingly found themselves in financial bondage to the community's wealthy. Samuel Lemon, only too pleased to grant such notes of credit to workers beholden to him, could cash them in for full value with the railroad. There is an obvious relationship between that unhealthy situation and the "absenteeism, insubordination, and insobriety" that was noted among the workers. Also it's no wonder that one "well-disposed citizen" complained of the "drunken revelry . . . nightly scenes of intoxication" among the workers. One suspects that those "bacchanalians among the indigent laborers" were more desperate than frivolous.

The toll of maimings and accidents at the lowest level of work was frightful. This was true also, of course, among the passengers (who might be called willing victims of the Portage Railroad). In a three-day period in June 1834 there was a particularly spectacular series of accidents. In one of them a car at the head of Plane One broke loose and, "descending with inconceivable velocity," smashed into the posts of the shed at the foot. The only passenger, "a respectable stranger," was hurled 60 feet through the air into the Conemaugh River. Although railroad personnel were able to fish him out swiftly, he died the following evening from a fractured skull.

Other passengers enjoyed happier journeys, among them Charles Dickens, who made the trip in 1842. His description of the experience is a high point of American canal literature.

It was pretty travelling thus at a rapid pace along the heights of the mountains and with a keen wind, to look down into a valley full of light and softness and catching glimpses through the treetops . . . and we riding onward high above them like a whirlwind.

But before that section of his journal, Dickens took the trouble to reassure travelers who might follow him that the Allegheny Portage Railroad was not as dangerous an experience as they might have heard:

On Sunday morning, we arrived at the foot of the mountain, which is crossed by railroad. There are ten inclined planes; five ascending and five descending; the carriages are dragged up by means of stationary engines; the comparatively level spaces between them being traversed sometimes by horse and sometimes by engine power as the case demands. Occasionally the rails are laid upon the extreme verge of a giddy precipice and looking from the carriage window, the traveler gazes sheer down without a stone or scrap of fence between into the mountain depths below. The journey is very carefully made however, only two

203

carriages traveling together and while proper precautions are taken, it is not to be dreaded for its dangers.

When he arrived at the summit, Dickens doubtless stayed at Lemon House. There he would have spent 25 cents for the night, and another 25 cents for each meal consumed; a whiskey punch would have cost him half that amount. He undoubtedly met Samuel Lemon and his wife and two daughters, all of whom participated in the great business of entertaining the stream of visitors, famous and otherwise. (A visitor of a different species, some years after Dickens, was "Old Whitey," President Zachary Taylor's horse, who accompanied the corpse of his master on the funeral voyage from west to east.)

Samuel Lemon had been born in Lancaster County, Pennsylvania, in 1793, and concluded as a young man, after service in the army, that riches would flow to those who paid attention to the business of building a transportation industry across the state. His first move in the region had been to buy 200 acres and assemble a log tavern at a good location down on the turnpike. There he began to prosper, and to keep his ears open about where and how the impossible-sounding Main Line Canal would get itself over the mountain. When he heard about the survey of 1831 and the course of the route, he moved swiftly to buy property at the head of Plane Six. There in 1832 he built his imposing stone structure, which served as tavern, home, and business office.

The sagacity of Samuel Lemon benefits today's visitors to the Allegheny Portage Railroad National Historic Site: his tavern remains a place of spacious welcome, offering superb views and pertinent exhibits. One can still see, out front, the stone sleepers on which the rails rested; it's easy to imagine the crowds of people debarking, embarking, crowding through these rooms, inquiring about schedules, taking one last drink before departing. Park Service plans call for the reconstruction of a full-scale train, with sectional boats atop the flatcars, which should make this illusion all the more credible.

Some while ago the Park Service had another creative idea: to prepare a driving tour that would allow visitors to gather the physical impression, as they drove from point to point, that they, too, were ascending and descending on the railroad, in company with the canal-riders of the last century. Unfortunately, this proved to be one of those ideas more ingenious than safe (rather like the Portage Railroad itself); the state police expressed heavy doubts about letting automobile traffic on the major and minor roads of the region be subject to the fits and starts of tourists' curiosity. So the tour was never officially published.

But you can still do it on your own. That is, if you get in your imagined section canalboat (actually your car) at the Lemon House summit and leave the highway to take sinuous Route 53 down the mountain's west side through the towns of Lilly and Portage, you'll experience some of the high-flying thrills that Dickens wrote about. More instructively, you'll learn through the seat of your pants and from the sudden downslant of the car the the relationship between the gentle "levels" and the steeper "planes." The towns encountered here grew up—shacks and stores and churches—in direct response to the Portage Railroad; the town of Portage was a refueling station for the locomotives. As might be expected, lumbering (for fuel) was one of the regions' fast-blooming subindustries; those who found jobs for themselves as "wood haulers" were among the fortunate who earned the golden $1 a day.

Fascinating and impressive as the Portage Railroad is, both in what one may see today and in the readily imaginable steam engines of the past, there's something else that seems disturbing here. This is not the spectrous memory of the drunks or the maimed or the immigrants condemned to the poorhouse—they should be regarded, perhaps, as expected elements of a society advancing into the Age of Progress. No, this focuses on the basic carelessness that underlies the inventiveness of the Portage Railroad. It's the cursed nineteenth-century attitude of "Let's see if we can build it and make money from it, and the devil with the environmental or human consequences."

It's unbecoming, admittedly, for a twentieth-century critic to take shots at nineteenth-century mores. But we have a right, perhaps even an obligation, to consider the consequences of national attitudes, and in this location we find one of America's greatest (and often forgotten) tragedies, caused indirectly by what might be called the philosophy of the Portage Railroad. The Johnstown Flood of 1889, in which more than 2,200 were killed and $17 million worth of property was lost, came about not only because of the burst dam at a lake originally built as a water reservoir for the railroad. It also came about because of the extra water flow from hillsides recklessly denuded of timber for use on that railroad and other industries; this was the water that filled the lake that broke the dam.

On the wet afternoon of May 31, 1889, inhabitants of the bustling city of Johnstown—which had begun to prosper as an important junction of the Grand Canal in 1834 and grew to a manufacturing center—heard a low rumble that grew to a "roar like thunder." The South Fork Dam had burst, sending 20 million tons of water crashing down the narrow valley of the Little Conemaugh.

At the leading edge of the 36-foot-high wall of water cascading at 40 miles an hour toward the city churned a mass of masonry, rocks, and other debris. This succeeded in crushing "houses like eggshells" and in throwing locomotives around "like so much chaff." Many of the victims, swept up against a stone railroad bridge that would not give way, died an agonized death in coils of barbed wire released from one of the local factories. Others were consumed in the fires that raged through the ruins and the oily waters; still others died in the typhoid epidemic that followed the flood.

Again, the point of this from the perspective of American canal technology is that though canals might not have seemed landscape-damaging at first, further "progress" (meaning the addition of higher-tech elements such as wood-consuming steam power) prompted further destruction. The rinky-dink mode of construction, the by-guess-or-by-God approach to canal-building epitomized by the Allegheny Portage Railroad, might accurately be called ruthless now that we can see it at a distance.

Ruthless too was the attitude of the triumphant Pennsylvania railroad financiers when they acquired the state's canal system in 1844, just ten years after the Grand Canal's Opening. The railroad men shut down the several sections of the canal with impressive speed, giving little thought to which waterways might survive and serve in subsidiary roles. The Allegheny Portage Railroad—which, as one Pennsylvania historian pointed out, did after all do "the job it was built to do"—was swiftly replaced by the continuous rails of a steam-powered railroad, product of the Pennsylvania Railroad Company, founded in 1847.

Ultimately this strategic part of the state's mountainous landscape was conquered by the Pennsy's famous Horseshoe Curve. That gigantic masterpiece of landscaping and engineering has long been considered vital to

U.S. transportation. When German saboteurs were landed on our shores during World War II and captured soon thereafter, it was discovered that one of them had been assigned to blow up the Horseshoe.

History and Myth on the C&O

Just as driving down along the line of the Portage Railroad gives one a strange body-sense of participating in the excitements of that era, so does hiking or bicycling along the towpath of the Chesapeake and Ohio Canal. This canal parallel to the Potomac, it will be recalled, was the way in which Maryland, as a matter of state ambition, tried to leap the Appalachians and command western emigration and trade. It was also the grandchild of George Washington's long-desired Patowmack Canal. But, despite its ancient origins and its many decades of excellent service as a regional canal, it never made it as a major, national route West. Now, however, it does serve nobly as a national park, offering recreational delight to millions.

It was no accident that the Maryland company to build the canal got itself organized at just the time of the Erie's completion (1824–25); Baltimore was not going to be left out of the race to be the West's Atlantic port. The canal-planners, who called themselves the Chesapeake and Ohio Canal Company, soon made the decision to avoid totally Washington's slave-power-dug waterway around the Potomac River's Great and Little Falls. (Actually, by 1824 the old canal had been extended all the way up to the junction with the Shenandoah River, at Harper's Ferry.) They would build a completely new channel on the north side of the river, from the nation's capital to the coal city of Cumberland, Maryland, then over the mountains to the Monongahela River near Pittsburgh, 341 miles in all. A tunnel more than 4 miles long could take care of the mountains, they assumed. Their daring, impractical plan won the approval of both the U.S. Congress and the Maryland state legislature.

Many lost lives and $12 million later, the canal had reached and had stopped at Cumberland, 185 miles. From the day in 1828—you know which day, July 4—when President John Quincy Adams had turned the first shovelful of soil for the canal (actually, the second shovelful; he struck a root on the first attempt and had to try again) until completion in 1850,

207

twenty-two years of muscle and sweat were required, a record for American canals. A major factor in the construction delays was that planners of the Chesapeake and Ohio had to stuggle for land along the route against the equally ambitious builders of the Baltimore & Ohio Railroad.

On the very day when President Adams did his shoveling on the C&O Canal, construction also began on the B&O Railroad in Baltimore. It was a classic, no-holds-barred race of competing transportation means—although, initially, the Baltimoreans had merely intended to lay a track (for horse-drawn cars) from their city to Washington, expecting thereby to take freight from the end of the C&O to the coast. Obtaining authorization from the legislature, the railroad builders then decided to press on through Frederick, Maryland, to Point of Rocks on the Potomac. From there up the valley to Cumberland (the valley being tightly squeezed at many points between high banks) they intended to fight the canal-builders for every precious inch of roadbed. Legal battles between the two companies stopped all construction for four years, but finally the courts ruled in the canal-builders' favor. Nevertheless, the Baltimore & Ohio Railroad reached Cumberland eight years ahead of the canal.

What the builders of the C&O had to overcome, as well as the landscape and the legal hassles, was a total rise from tidewater to Cumberland of 610 feet, up over the continental fall line. And although the Potomac River would generally supply adequate water to fill the canal, elaborate waste weirs, two-hundred culverts, and eleven stone aqueducts had to be built to manage the hydraulics of carrying the waterway safely across the rugged landscape. Most troublesome of the construction projects was the 3,118-foot Paw Paw Tunnel, which took the canal beneath the foot of a Catoctin Mountain.

The designers called for a channel 50 to 60 feet wide at towpath level and 30 to 40 feet wide at the bottom of the ditch; depth would be 6 feet. There would be seventy-four lift locks, each of them 15 feet wide and 90 feet long. These would just have room for the standard canal barges, whose 92-foot length could be squeezed in them if the rudder was swung tightly up against the stern. Barges of that size could carry 135 tons of cargo, though 120 tons of coal was the usual load.

Also contributing to the slowness of construction was a lack of workmen in the area. Instead of slaves, the C&O's builders had to bring in immigrant workmen—mostly Germans and Irishmen, who fought each other bitterly. Then came miserably humid summers in which mosquitoes did their deadly work, bringing malaria, for which there was still no known cure. Under these circumstances, work often slowed to a complete halt.

Nonetheless, the work was well done, the masonry work superior, and the ditch walled off successfully from the raging river beside it. Of particular note for visitors to the canal today are the exquisite lock tender's houses. Built of stone to a standard design, these handsomely proportioned whitewashed structures vary from each other only in number of chimneys, one or two. Abandoned now, they offer pleasant homes for snakes and possums.

Although the completed C&O—so expensive, so long in the building—never could become a financial success, the canal served for many years as a competent carrier of passengers westward and coal eastward. Despite the roaring, whistling railroad trains alongside the canal route (and the fights between canallers and railroaders were fierce in early times), the carriers learned to get along with each other. Indeed, in the final years of its life, the canal was effectively owned by the railroad, whose directors strove to keep it going just as long as possible.

It was actually the floods and costs of maintenance that did the C&O in, more than the railroad. Tropical Storm Agnes of 1972, which made an ocean of the Potomac Valley and washed away canal banks as if they had never been built, was a modern reminder of the destructive tempests that have traditionally swept through this region. Perhaps the greatest of them all was the titanic flood of 1889, the year when the lake above Johnstown filled and burst. It remains something of a wonder, therefore, that the canal served the region so faithfully for so long, assisting the agricultural growth and the industrial strengths of the mid-Atlantic states until the rather typical flood of 1924.

This says nothing about the quality of life—the definite social accelerations—that valley people experienced as the canal began to work its magic. That lively record can be read in documents treasured by historical societies of such very special canal towns and cities as Williamsport and Sharpsburg, Maryland, and Shephardstown, West Virginia. Until recently in these and other communities oldsters could bring the canal era back to life in a few phrases and images. Some of these reminiscences have been collected in an exemplary book of regional lore, *Home on the Canal* by Elizabeth Kytle. The title comes from a memorable statement made by one of the interviewees, Benjamin Garris. He reported, "I do believe that [most boatmen along the canal] really enjoyed it. It was their living. It was home."

This hometown, up and down a valley where there had been but scarce development before the canal, sang and marched to the tune of the boatmen and lock tenders. It was a rough-and-tumble middle- and lower-class life, so structured that the men and women who did the toughest work ended up with the least for their lives. When Evelyn Pryor, who grew up on her father's canalboat, was asked about her life, she said that she had hated leaving Williamsport each springtime to ship down the canal. But she had to, to do her father's cooking. And each year, having overcome her homesickness, she got used to the shipboard pattern again.

A high moment came for her once when she had the thrill of seeing one of the other class of people, one of those privileged to save their money and to live in a big house and pay others to do the work. This mogul was Mr. George Nicholson. Having asked her father's special permission, young Evelyn went along to observe the payment process, to see the almost legendary Mr. Nicholson in action:

I imagine maybe he was 35 or 40, something like that. He was nice looking—big tall thin man. Very nice man. But as far as seeing inside the paymaster's boat, no canal man I don't think ever got to see in it. . . . The only way I could describe the payboat is—it was something like a yacht, but it wasn't that big.

The remembered elegance stayed her the rest of her life, as did memories of getting up at 4:30 every morning to make the breakfasts, and memories of the drownings, the drunks, the gleaming mules, the faithful pets and friends. She left it all behind as soon as she could get some high school education and leave the canal. She had seen all those families, generation after generation of them, stuck in the same jobs, which, despite the charms of canalside life, were brutal and humiliating. She ran away from her canal home, but she would never forget it.

In the opinion of another interviewee, Jacob Myers, who left the canal to sign up with the B&O Railroad, even work on the railroad was more rewarding that work on the canal. He concluded that the sentimentalizing about the C&O Canal was all quite misplaced, given its lack of financial success and the conditions along it. "That damned old canal's been a joke ever since it started," he declared.

Canals for Recreation

Whether remembered harshly or fondly, the C&O has enjoyed a splendid twentieth-century re-creation. A slender, inviting greenway, some of it watered, now stretches along the old canal route between Cumberland, Maryland, and the nation's capital. Credit for the Chesapeake and Ohio Canal National Historic Park is generally given to the late Supreme Court Justice William O. Douglas. It was he who, by challenging a decision of the press and staging a dramatic hike, convinced the reigning powers of the day that they should not build a parkway for automobiles along the route. The scenic highway had been promoted by certain regional planners who believed that, somehow, increased numbers of Sunday drivers out gawking at the now-sleepy canalside towns would stir things up and bring about a kind of Gasoline Alley renascence. Justice Douglas saw the foolishness of that plan.

Instead, he urged Washingtonians and Marylanders to realize that the demise of the C&O Canal left them with an opportunity to enjoy the magnificent wildlife that had by then moved back into the area. Enraged by an editorial in the *Washington Post* that had supported the autoway, he wrote an eloquent refutation in January 1965. His letter sang of the valley's "strange islands and promontories," its populations of "muskrats, badgers, and fox," the "whistling wings of ducks" over it. Furthermore, he challenged the editorial writer to backpack with him down the full length of the old canal, to see and hear what could never be observed from the window of a moving car.

In the seven days of that hike, two writers from the *Post* and others who accompanied the energetic Justice concluded that the area was indeed of overwhelming historical and natural value. The paper changed its stance, and soon the C&O Canal Association was formed to see to the creation of a national historic park—accomplished, most fortunately, in 1971. As a result, and because of the sensitive re-creation of the waterway and its surroundings by the National Park Service, an unmatched, mysterious, wild, but man-shaped landscape now beckons to potential explorers. These include not only hikers and bikers but also canoeists and campers, as well as picnickers and horseback riders. For all of them, the NPS has provided guidance and historical clues but no heavy-handed management. The visitor feels a wonderful freedom to take it or leave it, as he or she will.

The Park Service also deserves a share of the credit for the park's very creation. As far back as 1938 (soon after the destructive flood of 1936 and the sale of the canal to the U.S. government), the NPS succeeded in restoring and rewatering the section of the canal between Washington and Seneca. To do this, and to hold the line in other sections as well, it had to fight a continuing battle against local vandals and others who saw only the potential for trash where there were now leaking locks, rusting machinery, and abandoned boats. By 1939 the NPS had won enough converts to establish the area as a public park. Then came the nearly disastrous parkway plan and the nick-of-time intervention by the Justice. For once, the people were served by their servants—and by the majesty of the scene itself.

The cause of historic canals, so vigorously promoted by the American Canal Society and its members, does not, of course focus exclusively on the C&O and other obviously important canals. Local or regional or national, short as the Farmington, long as the Black River, examples of worthwhile restoration can be found in all parts of the country. In many cases these slender threads of "shining water" with flanking trails and wildlife areas contribute significantly to the building of what have come to be called "greenways"—a splendid concept being promoted by urban planners today. Ohio's delightful Cuyahoga Canal, between Akron and Cleveland, stands forth as the showcase of this concept in action.

Actually, restored canals have had their supporters for centuries, both here and abroad. Robert Fulton, it will be recalled, had written of a happy future time when canals would "pass through every vale, wind round each hill, and bind the whole country together in the bonds of social intercourse." That dream of employing the canals not only for economic improvement but also for bringing the people together in greater social harmony has ancient roots in our republic. And the dream has never faded.

A generation ago, a historian looking at a nearby canal that was wasting away from woeful neglect wrote:

There is little reason why at least a part of the state-owned Pennsylvania Main Line Canal should not have been maintained in operation to this day, for supplementary commercial as well as for recreational uses, serving to keep communities from the ugly isolation that is now standard, and to add that perfectly real charm to natural landscape which controlled water never fails to provide, whether in millrace, dam reservoir, canal, cultivated riverside, or duck-pond.

This Pennsylvania historian was far more interested in the commercial and recreational values of canals-made-parks than in their potential as conveyors of history and myth. A writer for *Nicholson's Guide to the Waterways of Great Britain's Northwest Region,* by contrast, wrote:

Large numbers of people are beginning to realize what a minority has known for a long time: that in the bustling, noisy, dangerous world, the canals provide a unique antidote to so much that annoys, bores, and disturbs us. A 2,000-mile network woven across the country, the rural canals are a part of the English landscape and a part of our history. Quiet and dignified, the rural canal with its charming bridges, archaic locks, and colourful boats has achieved a unity with, and enhancement of, the countryside. . . . The contrast between rural and urban canals is dramatic, for it is in a town that the canal affords a rare and rewarding glimpse of the [early] Industrial Revolution.

Echoing that same sentiment in our own country, the classic painter of New England scenes Eric Sloan wrote of how he spied with so much pleasure the Farmington Canal "disappearing back into the landscape." Yet, fortunately, many canals are not disappearing at all. Still parts of the natural scene, though man-made, they have been sensitively kept alive as reminders of a time when human sweat and rude shovels and black powder wrought useful sculptures—not industrial devastation—upon the land. They remind us also of that critical time in national history when an apparently irreversible decision was made to press ahead to the very limits of a given technology, and beyond.

Canals give us an opportunity to walk or float back along routes not taken. Routes not taken—the way of balance between agriculture and

213

industry, the less secular way, the more equal way between men and women—routes not taken but nonetheless once considered, here. By rediscovering the evocative magic of canals and the mythic people who created them and worked along them, Americans have an opportunity to reclaim a vital connection with the water-land of their birth. One step at a time, with mule and rope and boat, at 4 miles an hour, we enter the zone of our origins, horseflies and all.

ACKNOWLEDGMENTS

GATHERING the research for this book involved something more than driving up and down the Mohawk Valley several times and out to Buffalo once or twice—plus a glorious sail down the New York State Barge Canal. In the more disciplined research sessions that also occurred, the author read appropriate documents under the direction of curators and other staff members of the many excellent local historical societies and the national and state parks along the route of the Erie. It was their scholarship, their collections and recollections, that the author has been privileged to bring together in these pages. But the sheer fun of being on the Erie Canal and on and about the other mentioned canals will not be gainsaid, either; that was an important element in conceptualization and fulfillment.

The inspirational power of those travels was doubled for the author by the company of Miriam Anne Bourne, eminent wife and researcher, who died before the book's completion. Her fascination with the canalside societies of New York, Pennsylvania, Maryland, and the southern New England states informs the book with authenticity and life. Other guides to the present-day recreational delights of the Erie Canal were Claire and Ted Curtis of Rochester, Peter Wiles of the Mid-Lakes Navigation Company in Skaneateles, and Ray and Dottie Rogers of waterways everywhere.

There were also many professional associates and friends who insistently steered the author into new and pertinent areas of regional history. Among them were Don Wilson of the Erie Canal Museum in Syracuse; Ruth and John Bowen of Canandaigua, New York; William Shank, president of the American Canal Society; Eric Swenson and Jim Mairs of W. W. Norton; and Patricia Fowler of the Witherle Memorial Library, Castine, Maine (who rested not until the author had read Samuel Hopkins Adams's *Grandfather Stories*).

In the search for and acquisition of pictures, Liz Meryman of New

York was of great, professional assistance. Also helpful on the picture front were: Susan Myers, National Park Service; Mary F. Bell, Buffalo and Erie County Historical Society; Charles Stern, Billerica Historical Society; Gordon Gay, C&O National Monument; Brenda J. Wetzel, State Museum of Pennsylvania. To them all, the author extends his gratitude.

Chapter One

The Lowell (Massachusetts) National Historic Park deserves special thanks for helping the author arrive at an understanding of the sociogeographical context within which the Erie Canal phenomenon occurred. Similarly, the historical societies of western and central New England—specifically those of South Hadley and Holyoke, Massachusetts, and Windsor, Connecticut—deserve warm thanks for their cordial and effective assistance. The author is grateful to Lawrence Coolidge for his perception of the relevance of France's Canal du Midi to the Erie, and to Sarah and Jonathan Bourne for their similarly strong advocacy of the Middlesex Canal; also to Andrew Bourne for his in-the-field photographic skills.

Chapter Two

At the New York State Museum in Albany, Craig Williams introduced the author to the wealth of Clintoniana that exists before and behind the scenes; for that intriguing glimpse, as well as for a survey of the museum's picture collections, much gratitude much be expressed. And to Mark Klimck of the Little Falls Historical Society—which is housed in a gemlike Greek Revival bank—special thanks are owed for his courtesy and for a candid tour of that key city's past and present. Other local historical societies also offered helpful views of social and technological evolution across three centuries in these New York valleys; particularly outstanding were the museum at Fort Hunter near the Erie's Schoharie Crossing and the Herkimer Home downstream from Little Falls. The author also salutes the staffs of such sites as Fort Stanwix National Monument and Guy Park near Fort Johnson for their lively recreations of regional history.

Chapter Three

The archive of the Canal Museum at Easton, Pennsylvania (Lance Metz, Historian), publishes a series of scholarly papers on American canals and also provides impeccable guidance to researchers in this field. Premier among popular, canal-focused museums, the Erie Canal Museum, housed in the former weighlock at Syracuse, is exemplary for both its educational outreach programs and its patient assistance to visiting writers. Less grand but no less well focused, local operations such as the Canastota Canal Town Museum near Chittenango impart a strong sense of just-yesterday. Sincere thanks are also expressed to Robert Howard, Curator for Engineering at the Hagley Museum near Wilmington, Delaware, for his explanation of nineteenth-century explosives.

Chapter Four

At Lockport, explorers in search of social history find not only the collections of the Niagara County Historical Society but also the Colonel Bond House and an extraordinarily helpful Chamber of Commerce, whose historian, Howard Colby, is a treasure chest of cultural information. At Rochester both the Historical Society (Ms. Elizabeth Holahan, Director) and the Landmark Society of Western New York (Cynthia Howk, Architectural Research Coordinator) offer in-depth facilities for studying the full range of canalside living. The author wishes to express his gratitude for the hospitality and assistance extended to him at these and other deservedly proud upstate New York facilities.

Chapter Five

The author was accorded close-up views of the working of today's New York State Barge Canal thanks to the many kindnesses of Thomas J. Ryan of the State Canal Board and Thomas M. Prindle of the Waterways Division of the State Department of Transportation.

Popular and scholarly facilities also await researchers at canal locations beyond New York State. For the story of the Lehigh and Morristown canals, Hugh Moore Park at Easton, Pennsylvania (Richard Ellis, Chief Interpreter; Carle J. Kopecky, Historian) is an incomparable source. For Pennsylvania's Main Line Canal, researchers are advised to spend time in the libraries of the Pennsylvania Historical Society and the Philadelphia Atheneum before going out to discover the rich resources of such installations as Allegheny Portage Railroad National Historic Site (Larry Trumbello, Chief Interpreter) or Johnstown Flood National Monument. To comprehend the many-faceted social and technological history of the

Chesapeake and Ohio Canal, travelers along its length may find historical societies in many of the canal towns, including Shepherdstown and Harpers Ferry, West Virginia, where the National Parks facility succeeds in putting the canal and the railroad into the perspective of the entire span of American history.

It is the author's hope that the men and women at the above libraries and museums will feel that the generosity of their contributions to this book has been repaid to some extent by its qualities, and also that all those who made similar contributions but were unintentionally omitted from this listing will find here some reason for forgiveness.

BIBLIOGRAPHY

Adams, James Truslow. *New England in the Republic, 1776–1850*. Boston: Little, Brown, 1926.

Adams, Samuel Hopkins. *Grandfather Stories*. New York: Random House, 1947.

Andrist, Ralph K. *The Erie Canal*. New York: American Heritage, 1964.

Anonymous. "Canals, Navigation, and Commerce on the Connecticut River." South Hadley, Mass.: South Hadley Historical Society, 1978.

———. *Nicholson's Guides to the Waterways—Northwest Region*. London: Nicholson Publications, 1988.

Baker, Anne Kathleen. *A History of Old Syracuse*. Fayetteville, N.Y.: 1941.

Bannan, Theresa, MD. *Pioneer Irish of Onondaga (About 1776–1847)*. New York: Putnam's, 1911.

Blake, Nelson Manfred. *A Short History of American Life*. New York: McGraw-Hill, 1982.

Bliven, Bruce, Jr. *New York: A History*. New York: W. W. Norton, 1981.

Bobbe, Dorothie. *De Witt Clinton*. New York: Minton, Balch, 1933.

Burns, James MacGregor. *The Vineyard of Liberty*. New York: Knopf, 1982.

Carey, Matthew. *Brief Review of the System of Internal Improvement of the State of Pennsylvania*. Philadelphia: 1831.

Carmer, Carl. *Listen for a Lonesome Drum*. New York: Farrar & Rinehart, 1936.

———. *The Hudson*. New York: Rinehart, 1939.

———. *The Farm Boy and the Angel*. Garden City, N.Y.: Doubleday, 1940.

Clarke, Mary Stetson. *The Old Middlesex Canal*. Easton, Pa.: Center for Canal History and Technology, 1974.

Clayton, W. W. *History of Onondaga County*. Syracuse, N.Y.: 1878.

Coleman, John F. *Life and Labor Along the Allegheny Portage Railroad*. Cresson, Pa.: Allegheny Portage Railroad NHS, 1980.

Cross, Whitney R. *The Burned-Over District: The Social and Intellectual History of Enthusiastic Religion in Western New York, 1800–1850*. New York: Harper Torchbooks, 1950.

Di Carlo, Ella Merkel. *Holyoke-Chicopee: a Perspective*. Holyoke, Mass.: Transcript Telegram, 1982.

Drago, Henry Sinclair. *Canal Days in America*. New York: Clarkson Potter, 1972.

Dwight, Timothy. *Travels in New England and New York*. 4 vols. (reproduction of 1821 edition). Cambridge: Harvard Univ. Press, 1969.

Eaton, Deacon M. *Five Years on the Erie Canal*. Utica: Bennet, Backus, & Hawley, 1845.

Edmonds, Walter. *Rome Haul*. Boston: Little, Brown, 1929.

———. *Erie Water*. Boston: Little, Brown, 1933.

———. *Drums Along the Mohawk*. Boston: Little, Brown, 1939.

Ellis, David M.; James A. Frost; Harold C. Syrett; and Harry J. Carman. *A History of New York State*. Ithaca, N.Y.: Cornell University Press, 1967.

Ellsworth, Richard C., ed. *From Canton to Rochester: Canal Diary of Elisha Risden (1838)*. Rochester: Publication Fund Series, 1928.

Fanati, Edward E. *A Brief Account of the Windsor Locks Canal*. Windsor Locks, Conn.: 1976.

Finch, Roy G. *The Story of New York Canals: Historical and Commerical Information*. Albany: Office of State Engineer, 1925.

Freedgood, Seymour. *The Gateway States*. New York: Time-Life Books, 1967.

Fulton, Robert. *A Treatise on the Improvement of Canal Navigation*. London: I. & J. Taylor, 1796.

Garrity, Richard. *Canal Boatman: My Life on the Upstate Waterways*. Syracuse, N.Y.: Syracuse University Press, 1977.

Goodrich, Carter. *Canals and American Economic Development*. Port Washington, N.Y.: Kennicut Press, 1961.

Hahn, Thomas F. *Chesapeake and Ohio Canal Old Picture Album*. Shepherdstown, W. Va.: American Transportation Center, 1976.

Hamlin, Talbot. *Greek Revival Architecture in America*. New York: Dover, 1944.

Hand, M. C. *Syracuse: From a Forest to a City*. Syracuse, N.Y.: Myers & Stone, 1889.

Harlow, Alvin F. *Old Towpaths*. New York: Appleton, 1926.

Hayden, Roger, ed. *Upstate Trails—British Views of Nineteenth Century New York*. Syracuse, N.Y.: Syracuse University Press, 1982.

Judd, Sylvester. *History of South Hadley*. Springfield: 1905.

Kytle, Elizabeth. *Time Was: A Cabin John Memory Book*. Cabin John, Md.: 1976.

———. *Home on the Canal*. Cabin John, Md.: Seven Locks Press, 1983.

McBain, Howard Lee. *De Witt Clinton and the Spoils System in New York*. New York: AMS Press, 1967.

McCullough, Robert. *The Pennsylvania Main Line Canal*. Martinsburg, Pa.: Morrisons Cove Herald, 1962.

McKelvey, Blake. *Rochester, the Water-Power City 1812–1854*. Cambridge: Harvard University Press, 1945.

McPhee, John. *In Suspect Terrain*. New York: Farrar, Straus & Giroux, 1983.

Merk, Frederick. *History of the Westward Movement*. New York: Knopf, 1978.

Miller, Lillian B. *In the Minds and Hearts of the People*. Greenwich, Conn.: New York Graphic Society, 1974.

Muller, Alexis, Jr. *Looking Back, So That We May Move Ahead*. Lockport, Pa.: Sesquicentennial Committee, 1975.

Nagle, Paul C. *This Sacred Trust: American Nationality, 1798–1898*. New York: Oxford University Press, 1971.

Niven, John. *Martin Van Buren: The Roman Age of American Politics*. New York: Oxford University Press, 1983.

O'Donnell, Thomas C. *Snubbing Posts: An Informal History of the Black River Canal*. Boonville, N.Y.: Black River Books, 1949.

Redfern, Ron. *The Making of a Continent*. New York: Times Books, 1983.

Rinker, Harry L. *The Old Raging Erie . . . There Have Been Several Changes*. Berkeley Heights, N.J.: Canal Captain's Press, 1984.

Rolt, L.T.C. *From Sea to Sea: The Canal du Midi*. London: Allen Lane, 1973.

Schlesinger, Arthur M., Jr. *The Age of Jackson*. Boston: Little, Brown, 1946.

Shank, William H. *Vanderbilt's Folly: A History of the Pennsylvania Turnpike*. York, Pa.: American Canal and Transportation Center, 1964.

———, ed. *Towpaths to Tugboats: A History of American Canal Engineering*. York, Pa.: American Canal and Transportation Center, 1982.

———. *The Best from American Canals*. Vols. 1–4. York, Pa.: American Canal and Transportation Center, 1972–86.

Smith, Sabra. *Woodside's First Family*. Rochester, N.Y.: Rochester Historical Society, 1984.

Stiles, Henry R. *The History of Ancient Windsor*. Hartford, Conn.: 1891.

Strickland, William. *Report on Canals, Railways, Roads, and Other Subjects, Made to the Pennsylvania Society for the Promotion of Internal Improvements*. Philadelphia: H. C. Carey, 1826.

Thomas, Howard. *Black River in the North Country*. Prospect, N.Y.: Prospect Books, 1974.

Tobin, Catherine. "Irish Labor on American Canals." *Canal History and Technology Proceedings,* vol. 9. Easton, PA: 1990.

Waiger, Bernard, ed. *New York: A Guide to the Empire State (WPA)*. New York: Oxford University Press, 1940.

Wall, Joseph Frazier. *Alfred I. Du Pont, the Man and His Family*. New York: Oxford University Press, 1990.

Van Slyke, Lyman P. *Yangtze: Nature, History and the River*. Reading, Mass.: Addison-Wesley, 1988.

Warner, Charles E., ed. *Picturesque Hamden*. Northampton, Mass.: 1891.

Whitford, Noble E. *History of the Canal System of the State of New York*. 2 vols. Albany: 1906.

Wilson, Don, ed. *Straight from the Horse's Mouth: Firsthand Accounts of the Erie Canal*. Syracuse, N.Y.: Eric Canal Museum, 1988.

Wisbey, Herbert A. *Pioneer Prophetess: Jemima Wilkinson, the Public Universal Friend*. Ithaca, N.Y.: Cornell University Press, 1967.

Wyld, Lionel D. *Low Bridge! Folklore and the Erie Canal*. Syracuse, N.Y.: Syracuse University Press, 1962.

INDEX

Page numbers in *italics* refer to illustrations.

227